WOMEN, HEROES & A DAWG

Diane Ford Craig

DIANE FORD CRAIG

Alaska Press Minneapolis

First Edition (softcover)

Published jointly by Alaska Press + Books2Buttons.com

*Real-life stories, memoir
book club, travel and humor*

Layout, vintage photographs, words
and songs by author except where noted.
All stories from memory;
historical accuracy not guaranteed.
First names and/or pseudonyms
sometimes used to protect privacy.
Photos taken spontaneously over a lifetime.
Please excuse some blurriness.

Pin buttons courtesy of *Books2Buttons.com*

Library of Congress Control No. 2024913985

ISBN 978-1-886921-00-9

Printed in the USA

10 9 8 7 6 5 4 3 2 1

WOMEN...

[You, too, could write this book.]

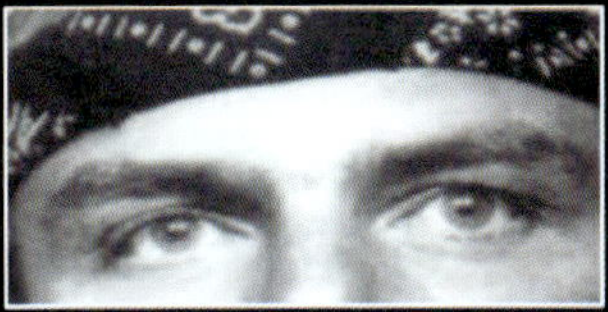

HEROES...

...and A DAWG

IN CAPTIVITY
I TEND TO
HALLUCINATE

Dedicated to

KELLY JANE FORD

(1966-2024)

(Never picked up.)

JAX

PUNCHLINE *(Song)*

Everything is open, the curtains are drawn
Children with their toy trucks are honking pretend horns
Cotton candy women in the latest pair of jeans
Sip fine wines on the steps of the latrine

Long silky spiders are slipping off to web
The unicorn has virgin found and is putting her to bed
Your mother's in the basement with a football helmet on
You're in the bathroom trying to turn on

Hot water, cold water, the story has begun
Wrapped in a towel, you give it to no one
You only know the bass line, so you sing it to the floor
While downstairs a lady laughs, trying to ignore

Filigreed atrocities bonded between her toes
Crystallized, anesthetized, she tries to blow your nose
If I only had a quarter for every toad I've kissed
I'd buy a shovel, start some trouble, nibble on your wrist

If you're looking for the punchline, then kindly step right in
And have a little lemonade with an unsuspecting friend
Sometimes I read the menu here, sometimes I turn a tear
And other times, I just sit right back and dig the atmosphere!

La-da-di-dah-lah-da, la-di-la-da-di-la...

Steve at The Cellar music venue & Castle Café, Cardigan, Wales

LIST OF STORIES

AN ADRIATIC INTRO

SILLY ME

Myrna, 84, always gets back on the horse – and still can!

SEEKING THE WORLD

LIST OF STORIES

SCARY STORIES

ART & MUSIC

Judy at the Corn Palace

THOUGHTFUL & INSPIRING

PARTING THOUGHTS

An Adriatic Intro

Dubrovnik, Yugoslavia (Croatia)

FOUAD & THE DEEP BLUE SEA

I always thought that if I wrote a book of my life stories, it would have to open with this one. Somehow, the picture of me resting innocently on a lawn chair on the back of an Adriatic ferry (and what came before and after) encapsulates my entire experience on this planet. But to get there, I have to start at the beginning, a beginning that also includes a boat tour. But this one is to the island of Korcula where Marco Polo was supposedly born. For an Orange County, California beach bunny perennially on a budget, this scenario is a long way from home.

But here I am.

Landing on the remote island not far from Dubrovnik, a tour guide splits us into separate groups where I meet two couples from Britain who tower over me. I swear they are 10 feet tall and twice as wide. I can't stop staring at them. Another man standing nearby strikes up a conversation with me in halting English. We find ourselves bonding over our inadequacies in the height department. Speaking mostly French, Fouad turns out to be a deeply tanned, jolly soul, just my

age, who has as much fun trying to communicate with me as I do with him. Somehow, based on personality alone, he jumps over my minimal education in the French language (two conversational classes and one in French folk singing) to the realm of complete understanding. As we share introductions, he tells me that he's come on this tour with a woman from Czechoslovakia who he barely knows, but she has been assigned to another group. In halting English, he also confides that he is a close cousin to the current president of Lebanon and that things are very heated in his home country.

FOUAD & THE DEEP BLUE SEA

Vacationing In Yugoslavia (Croatia) to laugh, play and eat, he says he is here to have fun. "Same here," I tell him and we settle into exploring the island together. (Later, at a library back home, I confirm that Fouad is actually Fouad which makes this memory just a tad bit more fun, at least for me anyway.)

Our conversations, a mixture of languages and hand gestures, are so entertaining that I quickly forget the existence of the mysterious other woman. There are churches and shops on the island but nothing that compares to Marco Polo's house, which is similar in style to an ancient fire tower: one room wide by about four stories high. I hope, for Marco's sake, that he scored the top floor for his bedroom with the grand ocean views. But the guide says that historians aren't quite sure which room was Marco's bedroom. So far, no one has actually *proven* that he was born here either. This makes the purpose of the tour (historically speaking) somewhat pointless, but still fun.

As the day wanes, Fouad asks me to meet him for dinner near the Dubrovnik drawbridge. I not only consent, I look forward to it. I am already familiar with the bridge because when I first arrived in Dubrovnik, my "suitcase on a leash," drew hoots of laughter from the old guys lining the bridge to watch the tourists. Paved with cobblestones, every few steps my suitcase would fall over on the walkway and one of the locals would run over and help me pick it up. It reminded me of the time I tried to ski Aspen, and was so bad at it, that I had to tack my way down the mountain like a sailboat. Dinner is fine, lots of red wine, roses and good food. The exchange rate is phenomenal, too, which makes it even better for both of us. Fouad pays the bill (which in American dollars would only have covered a single hamburger and fries at McDonald's not the lavish spread we enjoy tonight). After dinner, we walk the ancient streets of Dubrovnik holding hands like an old married couple. Being single, I am a free agent, but only consent to a glass of wine in his hotel room to enjoy the view of the sea. When we arrive, I notice a suitcase open on the floor containing what looks like, based on labels, canned food from Eastern Europe. My guess is that it belongs to the lady Fouad says missed the last ferry back; we will not be seeing her until morning.

Hmmmmm.

Laughing together until the early morning hours and singing songs in French about three happy ducks, we finally fall asleep until we are awakened by someone banging on the door. Maybe there was another boat after all? As I run to gather what little I have with me, Fouad begs me to agree to meet him the next day.

This I cannot do.

"So sorry, Fouad," I tell him. "My ferry leaves at 8 in the morning."

"No, please!" he says, struggling to find the right words in English as the banging on the door continues. "Stay here with me. We will have a wonderful time."

While it is flattering and fun to be so pursued (minus the sounds from the hallway, of course) I really do have a non-refundable ferry ticket to cross the Adriatic the next day; I can't afford to miss the boat.

Fouad encourages me to hide under the bed but I finally resort to telling a white lie: I will meet him for breakfast at the same restaurant by the drawbridge. Plans made, we run giggling to the door (for different reasons, I think) and, on the count of "un-deux-trois" (1-2-3), I run out into the hallway alone. Wishing the bewildered woman well, I make my way back to my room located by a picturesque church on a town square. I never do see Fouad again (that was our time) but even so, this is only part of the story.

Waking early, I make my way to the ferry and discover to my great excitement that although it is a tiny, little vessel (as ferries go), there is actually a swimming pool on the main deck! Surveying the ship and the other passengers, I try to find a good place to plop myself down in the sun with a book. The scene reminds me of how some people describe mullet haircuts: "Business in the front, party in the back." Across the pool (business), under the wheelhouse, maybe 50 people embodying the description "huddled masses" sit hunched together eating finger foods from well-worn paper bags. I try to make eye contact but they completely ignore me – and not one of them is smiling or wearing a bathing suit. Most likely itinerant workers commuting from Yugoslavia to Italy, they are clearly not happy about making the trip.

On the other side of the boat (party) where I am, there are many chairs and lots of breathing space. Yay! I have easy access to the pool and it looks like a nice, comfortable place to read a book. I pick out the best location next to a railing and, for security reasons as I've been taught by other travelers, use a handy metal clip to attach my backpack to it.

Stretching out on a cushy chaise lounge, I discreetly exchange my long black pants for my treasured travel skirt with the colorful print. For me, this scene is about as close to bliss as any traveler can dream of, knowing that for the next eight hours it will just be me, my book and the sun.

But this is not to be.

About an hour into the Adriatic, the sea swells. At first, the sensation is pleasant like the first few minutes on a waterbed – until *whee!* The sky darkens and waves take hold of the ship. Most of the time the huddled masses ignore me as the water in the pool creates little mini waves that are fun to watch. And then, we hit a big one, a big wave, and the masses look up from their breakfasts. Instead of looking at the pool and sky, they look directly at me! Why? Is my travel skirt hiked up too far on my thighs for them? Or is it something else? In slow motion,

FOUAD & THE DEEP BLUE SEA

Favorite travel skirt

I watch the pool water get sucked up into a wave like a mini tsunami, but then quickly retreat. When the next even bigger wave hits the ferry seconds later, all hell breaks loose. Not only does the pool water swell toward the masses, it reverses itself, breaks free and heads my way – knocking me off the chaise lounge, my book flying overboard, my travel skirt rising over my head, and the joy and excitement of being on the water changing to the fear of not having enough air left in my lungs to sustain life! When the wave finally subsides (a rogue wave, I presume), I pull my skirt from my face to survey the still-dry huddled masses and realize that I am totally and completely a party of one. Part of me still hopes that one of them might laugh or smile. But there is no laughter. In any language, "You dumb you-know-what" can be communicated without words. As the group stares at me from a position totally protected by the captain's wheelhouse, I realize that I am the only one on the deck who doesn't know the secret of the waves.

Regrouping in great humility, I nonchalantly re-cover my nakedness, smooth the wrinkles from my shirt, unearth a granola bar and Diet Coke from my wet (but intact) backpack, look up at the sky, and to my own surprise, laugh my heart out. Laugh? Really? I laugh so long and so hard that, once again, I can't catch my breath and I practically start snorting into the wind in front of God and everybody.

Surviving situations like these (even going out into the world and risking them), inspires me to write my stories. Each one is a tribute to the beauty and absurdity of this life we have been gifted to live, as Paul Simon says, "so well, so long."

Boots &
Betty

Silly Me!

Jim Bob

BLUEGRASS SHRIMP

To exist, rural electric companies sometimes require a bit of political lobbying. One year, when I am living in Alaska, my job is to set up an appealing and fun party to get politicians to support our causes in Juneau. Most companies go the traditional route to attract legislators but I want something different. In addition to all the usual bells and whistles, I book a well-known bluegrass band and excellent caterer to start things off. After the large banquet room is set up, I look out over my handiwork with pride and hope.

"This is gonna be one awesome party!" I think.

An hour before the doors open, the caterers set up a giant ice sculpture centerpiece that features about 500 jumbo shrimp, a touch sure to woo the crowd. The musicians, paid to start any minute, mill around looking longingly at the food. Seeing this, I suggest that they have a bite to eat to hold them through the evening. That done, I charge upstairs to change for the event and, when I return, everything still looks great. It's ready, set, go – until I notice a small gathering of people blocking my view of the ice sculpture. Pushing through the bodies, I find that the musicians have so enjoyed the shrimp display, they have helped themselves to almost every piece on the sculpture.

That's a lot of crustacean!

In a moment of truth almost every event planner knows, the world stops spinning. I can freak out, banish the musicians from the room and send the hotel staff scrambling to dig up last minute substitutes for food and music. Or, I can reach for the two remaining shrimp, dip them into the last of the cocktail sauce, joyously chomp them down and bank on the hope that the beauty of the ice sculpture itself, *sans shrimp* (and maybe with a lot of free alcohol?) might save the day. It does!

FASTER THAN MY FILTERS

Working at a soap company for a high-level executive named Sterling, he sometimes offers my services to his underlings because he travels a lot. The problem is, if the request requires leaving my desk, the Treasurer's executive assistant in the next cubicle has to cover our phones and can't leave her station. One day, listening to me trying to accommodate yet another request, she decides she's had enough. As a young comptroller half my age directs me to run paperwork across campus for the umpteenth time, she waits for him to leave and finally speaks up:

"Just ask the guy: 'Do you have two broken legs? Do you sit any closer to the elevator than I do?'"

One thing to know about my co-worker; her previous job was as head bunny for the Playboy Club in New York City. She is gorgeous. She is experienced. I once heard her ask someone higher on the food chain than my boss to trim her split ends and he did. Is this all about the clout of our bosses or my own personal assertiveness level? The next day, when the comptroller tries to get me to run his errands again, I give it my best shot:

"Do you have two broken legs?..."

Later that week – sitting across from him in a disciplinary meeting that he's demanded with my boss – the comptroller stares at me like I've confiscated his keys to the executive washroom. Nothing my boss says calms him down until, in a Solomon-like gesture, Sterling reaches for both of our hands and sings two verses (badly, I might add) of "Kumbaya, my Lord, Kumbaya."

Although I earn the respect and love of my Playboy bunny co-worker with this maneuver, I never attempt it again. I never had to! Maybe what her suggestion lacked in tact it made up for in efficacy? Maybe she was right after all?

SHELLY & THE GHOST OF GRANDMA PAST

As I write this story, today's date – June 14th – sets off a reminder bell on my inner birthday list. Grandma Margaret (aka The Black Rose) was born June 14, 1902. That would make her 123 years old today. Should I take this coincidence as a sign?

The drama level was often high in my parents' cul-de-sac home in Southern California.

"Better than TV!" Grandma used to say when she visited us from Boston. Holding court on the living room couch in a bulky leopard skin coat in mid-summer, Grandma munches a big bowl of buttered popcorn. Through thick black glasses, she watches 2 stressed parents, 2 beach bunnies, 2 football players and 2 toddlers stumble through their days together. Spying down on her through the slats of the main staircase in my pajamas once, I dub Grandma The Black Rose of the family.

Of course, I am nothing like her.

That is until I wake up one day in an office chair in Minnesota, bowl of popcorn on my lap, feeling like I need a new pair of glasses. There's been a switch in management at the soap company I work for. The Big Boss's assistant, a woman named Shelly, has assumed the unofficial role of Queen of the Forest. Her first official act is to install a window in the wall of her cubicle so that she can peer down the rows of subordinates to ensure that we are on the job. The problem is that we are all assistants to high-level executives with excellent track records and no official connection to her on the org chart.

SHELLY & THE GHOST OF GRANDMA PAST

Slowly, it also becomes evident that Shelly is taking her job so seriously, that she is documenting my movements. Why? Every day at 9:10 AM, she nonchalantly walks past my cubicle, stares in to make sure I am in my chair, and then, I assume, takes the circular route back to her desk.

Rinse and repeat daily!

One morning, I feel the need to test the reality of my observations. Donning the closest thing I have to a leopard-skin coat (reminiscent of you-know-who), I scoot my chair to the edge of my cubicle at 9:08 AM, face out and wait for the morning patrol. Minutes later, as Shelly's first foot comes into view, we lock eyes.

She freezes, I stifle laughter. Not knowing whether to run or hide, she turns around quickly and retraces her steps to her desk. She never checks on me again, at least at 9:10 AM, but not long after that, her boss (who I have not yet met in person), calls my boss into his office.

"Why do you keep your assistant?" he apparently asks him, probably not realizing that I've worked there 15 years with near-perfect reviews.

"Because she's good?" my boss answers. "Because she's always on time?"

After that, there is always a little extra cream in my boss's coffee – and yes, The Black Rose gets extra butter on her popcorn as well.

GINNY & THE HUNGRY WASP

George

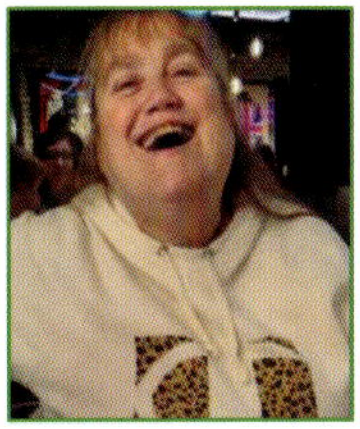

One night at Heartbreakers in Chaska, Minnesota (one of my husband's favorite music gig venues), a wasp repeatedly dive-bombs my friend Ginny's flatbread pizza – and us. Not sure what to do, we name him George and offer him a saucy crust on a salad plate to leave us alone.

George says no.

Upping the game (and not knowing if wasps are carnivorous), we try replacing the crust with a chunk of hamburger and cover the bigger pie with a napkin and a spoon.

Bingo!

For the next hour, George conducts a love affair with the snack – munching, rubbing and gnawing at it with apian gusto. Somehow, we get it right and Ginny gets to eat her pizza in peace.

Did you know that some bees and wasps recognize human faces? Maybe we'll meet George again someday!

WHERE'S THE FUDGE?

In 1979, I move to New York City and reconnect with Grandma Margaret ("The Black Rose") and the other rellies in Boston after a long absence. It's Easter season and I am surprised when Grandma herself rings me up.

"Go to Macy's basement today," she says, "and buy me some fudge."

"But you're diabetic, Grandma," I respond. "Is there something else you'd like a little better?"

"It's not for me," she answers. "It's for the …. nuns."

Since I live only a few blocks from Herald Square, I get right on it, only to be bewildered by the volume of holiday shoppers.

Standing in the middle of a basement aisle, I try unsuccessfully to locate the fudge department in all of the chaos.

"Hum, hum, hum," I hear in harmony behind me – two men dressed as daisies and another as a tulip are serenading me in three-part harmony. Smilingly, they direct me to where I need to go.

I love New York, you can never predict.

I soon reach the fudge department and when I do, wow, what a display. I want to buy a little of everything. But Grandma specifically stated "chocolate walnut fudge," and so I comply, shouting my order to the man across the display case like a real native New Yorker.

"How much do you want, lady?" he shouts back.

Good question! If I only buy one chunk for Grandma, there won't be enough for the other Boston relatives when I get there.

"Give me the whole thing," I say, going for the gold (which amounts to something like ten pounds of fudge the size of a half sheet cake). The purchase is way out of my budget but it's worth it to make Grandma, I mean the ladies at the convent, happy.

The train ride to Boston, as usual, is entertaining, but not half as entertaining as the reunion with Uncle Barney at the other end. Out of kindness, he offers to pick me up at the train station even though my first stop is with the other side of the family. A Boston cop who blasts Irish music on the radio at a dire pitch, he focuses his conversation on advising me how to stay safe in New York City:

"If anyone comes at you on the street, jump up on their waist, howl like a hyena and bite anything you can sink your teeth into."

"I might need a stepladder to do that," I tell him.

"Yeah, well, you might have to get one because you're a good-looking woman – but you're too gosh darn fat!" (Not his exact words.)

Ouch. This is a very rude thing to say to your niece, but in its own way, it is also kind of sweet. Barney is not only from the other side of the family, he's from another side of life. When his mother died a few years ago, he led me to her casket, gave her face a pinch and a slap, and said: "You're looking a little pale there, Ma."

"I love you, Uncle Barney," I tell him as he drops me at Grandma Margaret's apartment with my little weekender suitcase and the large pan of fudge. "But you're too gosh darn kind!"

"Safe home."

Grandma lives on the third floor of an apartment building In Revere, Massachusetts without an elevator, but I manage to get myself up there in record time. Throwing open her door, the first thing she says to me is, "Did you bring the fudge?"

"Got it right here, Grandma," I tell her as she grabs the pan, slaps it down on the kitchen table and pulls it out of the wrapping.

"Nice, nice," she mumbles quietly, gesturing over everything but a small slice of the entire pan. "I'll take this much."

Oh, sh--. I bought enough to gift everyone. How do I handle this? "How about THIS much?" I answer.

"Have you lost your hearing in New York?" she asks me, increasing her volume with every word. "I'll take THIS much, DIANE."

She knows my name!

Remembering that Grandma is maybe one year away from her final resting place (and fudge is just fudge), I slip the whole thing back into the bag and say, "It's all yours, Grandma. Do you want it gift wrapped?"

"Not necessary," she says. "I'll take it just like it is. I'm seeing the nuns tomorrow."

I'm not sure how much fudge those nuns can eat, but I do know that Grandma keeps our visit short and sweet that day and never offers me a single slice.

I guess Macy's fudge is that good.

Or maybe Grandma is?

Thank heavens our other grandma, Grandma Millie, was completely normal!

FRONT OR BACK?

The following 3 stories happened when I was 16, with two different best friends and a jolly gym teacher in Huntington Beach, California.

STORY #1

It's 1968, and my parents have recently moved our family to the West Coast from New Jersey. A good way to highlight my culture shock is by contrasting my experience in the girls' locker rooms.

At Immaculata High School in Somerville, New Jersey, showers are a connected, three-part, all-curtained process:

- Stall #1 is where one girl (me) steps in, pulls the curtain and disrobes.
- Stall #2 has the showerhead; you walk into it and shower.
- Stall #3 is where you dry off with the towel you stashed before undressing in Stall #1.
- Reverse: Walk back from Stall #3, through Stall #2, into Stall #1 to get dressed again.
- Done.

At Huntington Beach High School, the process is so simple, no bullet points are necessary: **All the naked girls line up at the entrance to the group showers, one tiny towel per girl, and with two coverage choices – *front or back?***

It's one of those situations when, if you make a fuss, it will follow you forever. So, I choose front, positioning the towel just below my belly button with my left hand, crossing the other arm over my boobs as best I can. Taking my place in line to get checked off by Ms. Gill, I can't believe I have to be naked in front of my gym teacher (not to mention all the other freshman girls) on the first day of my California high school career. And maybe daily for the rest of high school?

Ms. Gill is feeling quite chatty today.

"Name?"

"Diane Ford."

"Oh, you're the new girl, aren't you? I'll write you in."

"Yes."

"How are you liking Huntington Beach High School?"

I adjust my towel a little higher.

"Don't know yet."

Behind *my behind*, five other girls push to move the line along so that they can get back to the lockers to reattach their wiglets before lunch.

"I hope you enjoy Huntington Beach," Ms. Gill continues. "Where did you move from?"

"New Jersey."

"You'll love the beaches here, too. "

"Thanks."

"Next!"

Ugh.

That was January, but soon enough, summer comes.

STORY #2

I am young and – not bad – now living in the heart of the surfing capital of the world. Out on the water, my new friends, boys and girls, make surfing history with innovative moves and maneuvers that surfers in Hawaii still imitate today. History or no history, the beach is the thing and we spend every free waking moment there.

FRONT OR BACK?

Grabbing the last set of available car keys from a kitchen hook (the '59 Ford family station wagon), I make a beeline to the pier. Not wanting to parade the ugly family car past my friends, I park far, far away on a side street and walk back to the beach. Spearing my single car key to a $5 bill with my sisters' old diaper pin, I attach it inside the waist of my bathing suit bottoms, hoping it will not ruin the overall effect I am trying to achieve.

I am 16 and so is Debbie Dart, my best friend, who I'm set to meet in a few minutes by the pier. I like her because she is creative and thinks things through. She likes me, she says, because I am the class poet and have already done a lot of living we both spend hours trying to make sense of. Depth doesn't matter much here except if you are exploring the ocean. But on the beach, it's all fun and bikinis and I kind of like that.

After an idyllic day of sunbathing, body surfing and taco strips at Jack's on the sand, Debbie and I walk across the famous Pacific Coast Highway ("PCH") to Jack in the Box with our precious transistor radios for ice cream.

Carrying our prizes, we wait for the light to change on PCH in our $1 bikinis. Mine – a brown, white and black Mondrian pattern – probably looks pretty good on me. But it is never quite as elegant as Debbie's suits given that she has the touch with sewing machines and came up with the original idea of the $1 bikini in the first place.

Still waiting to cross, I decide to get a head start on the huge chocolate milkshake I've bought with babysitting money while waving at various boys and friends passing by in convertible MG sportscars, Woodies and Mustangs.

After New Jersey, this is the life!

Somewhat distracted, I position my thick straw above the perforated cardboard insert (a little "U" cut into the cup top that needs to be pressed open by the straw). I push – not too hard, not too softly. As the straw connects, the little "U" repels it, flips the top over and grabs a big chunk of chocolate ice cream on the way to my unsuspecting cleavage. Barring shark bites and jellyfish, this is one of the worst things that can happen to a young girl on the beach. I still remember the sensation of that cold, chunky liquid running down the front of my body, all the way to my toes in about the most visible public setting a beach bunny can imagine – maybe in the whole world! Debbie attempts to soothe my teenage vanity and clean me off with the one napkin we have between us. But I am forever mortified and nothing can make me feel better.

STORY #3

Fast forward to the same city and time frame, but not the beach. As luck would have it my other best friend Connie and I both land jobs at the local W.T. Grants (pre-Target). At the time, Connie is dating Elliott (eventually her husband) and I am more in love with newfound Mexican food and the beach than boys. Elliott and I tolerate each other (who knows why?) and I try not to talk to him for silly teenage girl reasons, I suppose. On this day, a work day at Grants, I stop at Don Jose's down the street for a lunch of chips and salsa, three cheese enchiladas, a side of beans and rice and a Diet Coke before work.

An important thing to know about our new jobs is that when W.T. Grants hired us, they got the departments completely wrong. Connie, a beautiful, slim blond (the offspring of an equally beautiful mother), is assigned – not to the women's fashion department as you would expect – but to the candy department! *What a waste!*

FRONT OR BACK?

And I – a lifelong candy expert and super modest graduate of 8 years of somewhat repressive Catholic grade school – am assigned to the underwear department! *Are you kidding me?* Underwear? I won't even go to a department store to buy underwear for myself. And so, I begin my new job constantly mortified but somehow bucking up and managing to sell "drawers" and "briefs" to my mother's generation and black lacy panties to weird old men.

On this day, bending over to fold inventory into bins from plastic bags, I curse myself for having Mexican food before work. I have been waiting for the department to clear out because I am feeling a little backed up – you know, the kind of backup that spawned the term "crop dusting?" Straightening the last pink training bra, along comes Elliott looking for his beloved Connie. But I don't see him coming in the momentarily empty department. Focused more on my insides, feeling like the time is *now*, I am just about to let loose when, seeing me bent over, Elliott decides to surprise me with his presence. He jams both pointer fingers into the two sides of my waist and, whoosh! Instant *Blazing Saddles*! The results are not only fragrant but *loud* – and even more embarrassing than having to chat with Ms. Gill butt-naked or wear a chocolate milkshake on my chest on the PCH. Don't let anyone tell you that over time you'll mature out of these humiliations. Fifty-three years later, I can still feel the acute, crimson flush of embarrassment – and I haven't looked Elliott or Ms. Gill in the face since!

Connie & Elliott Today

POPSICLES & SURGERY PLUS

I've just made it through recovery, feeling blissful, looking forward to a quiet room and maybe a popsicle or two – and wham! The orderly pushing my stretcher loses control and slams it into the wall of my room. The jolt doesn't bother me, as I am still so "happy" from the anesthetic. But then, in slow motion, I watch the TV above me separate from its mount, eventually landing on my bare legs.

I don't feel a thing.

In and out of consciousness, I think the TV looks somewhat odd down there, for sure. I don't mind a bit until I open my eyes again to see a circle of medical personnel surrounding my bed like on doctor TV when someone has just flatlined.

"Am I dead?" I ask fearfully.

Four nurses answer in suit:

#1: "No, honey! You're fine."
#2: "At least it wasn't your head!"
#3: "Lawsuit, anyone?"
#4: "To X-ray. Stat!"

As the tech lifts me from my warm, anesthetic-induced bliss onto a cold slab in the X-ray room, I am miserable for the first time here.

"Lawsuit? Really?" I finally say between takes. "All I need is an orange popsicle – lime if you have it – and maybe a cherry one after that?"

LUKE SKYWALKER IN HOT COFFEE

Luke Skywalker can protect himself against toxic aliens and invisible shields, but he is no match for my klutziness at a pool in Newport Beach.

On a star-studded summer day, I face a terrible dilemma. As a waitress at a fancy country club behind the Fashion Island mall, I have already served coffee to Pilar Wayne (John Wayne's wife) and the Queen of Sweden. I've hung out multiple times with Mr. Drysdale from The Beverly Hillbillies (asking his advice on my music career) while serving his wife Gabby her favorite Salad Nicoise.

This country club is a classy place and, at a fancy pool party like this, management breaks out the large silver coffee pots with the big arms and tells us to keep the java flowing after dinner.

Dressed in a frilly, low-cut, brown-and-beige outfit, I lean in to each customer, serve them coffee and then move down to the next person along the row.

Close seating like this creates serving challenges, especially on a sun-drenched

patio with VIP guests, but I do my best to keep going. I don't think much about it, though, caught up as I am with all the earthly stars and personalities surrounding me.

With the coffee pot in my right hand, I work one long table, sometimes exchanging niceties with stars like Mark Hamill, better known as Luke Skywalker of *Star Wars* fame. After I complete his fill, I take a step back, admiring his curly blond hair, when I realize that a strange pattern of long dark lines is developing on the sunny backs of the rich and famous.

"What's that?" I wonder to myself, studying the long, Chewbacca-colored

lines across some people's backs. Retracing my steps to investigate, I realize that I must have filled the pot too full. The coffee, having a mind of its own, is lightly spilling out on to summer jackets, shirts and dresses – but so far, no complaints. "It must not be hot enough to seep through and scald anyone," I think.

My natural inclination is to fess up, but if I do, it will cause a fuss and distract everyone from the party. Not to mention, I could lose my job.

"All's well, that ends well," Shakespeare wrote one time. I wonder if he also added "Whew!" at the end of it but kept it to himself?

Refilling my pot at the coffee station to a modest level this time, I fix a sunny smile on my face and get back to work. As a matter of continued employment, I'm learning that whatever happens, don't broadcast unfixable mistakes – just keep going!

THE COLOR OF MY FACE

One early morning in bed, waiting for the world to come alive in our newly acquired townhouse, I notice a few color glitches on our bedroom wall. Nothing horrific, mind you, just some well-placed touch-ups needed on one particular wall. Totally in new homeowner mode, I jump out of bed feeling confident and empowered. "I've got this," I think. "I am the woman for the job!"

Trying not to wake my husband, I grab an X-ACTO knife from a utility drawer and silently slice two coin-size paint chips from behind a red bookcase. Depositing the white speckles into a baggie, I toss them into my purse, grab my keys and point the family car toward Home Depot. Who else is open at this hour?

"Easy peasy," the sales clerk says cheerfully as I hand over the baggie with the paint chips. "I can match these for you in a jiffy."

"Yay!" I say, slapping her left hand with my right one like we are old friends.

Jumping higher than my dog Jax for chicken, she recoils like I've hit her, which of course, I would never do.

"Five minutes," she says. "And by the way, we aren't allowed to touch customers since Covid."

"But you could before?"

Within minutes, a small can of paint is shaking away in the shaking machine and I am headed home – me, the paint can and the coin chip baggie – well before most commuters hit the shower.

That afternoon, I lay newspaper on the floor, open the can of paint, dig up a cheap paintbrush and some paper towels, and get to work. But after a few strokes something is obviously wrong, very wrong. Instead of the institutional white color of my bedroom, this new paint is a creamy beige.

"Damn!" I yell when I realize the problem. Was the lady at Home Depot so mad at me for touching her that she gave me someone else's paint?" Working hard not to act like a Karen (since I am generally the right age and disposition), I try to look on the sunny side.

"All is not lost," I think. "Why not turn the whole wall with the glitches into a beige accent wall?"

Proud of myself for being so creative, I also add an interesting accent stripe and the end product looks good, great even – but also strangely familiar. Still needing the white touch-up paint for other areas, I rummage through my purse looking for the chip baggie to try again. But this time *two* baggies come up – one with the white coin-sized paint chips and the other containing swipes of brown makeup from a leaky foundation bottle. I must have given the lady at Home Depot the wrong baggie! But even better, I realize, I have just painted the bedroom wall the color of my face!

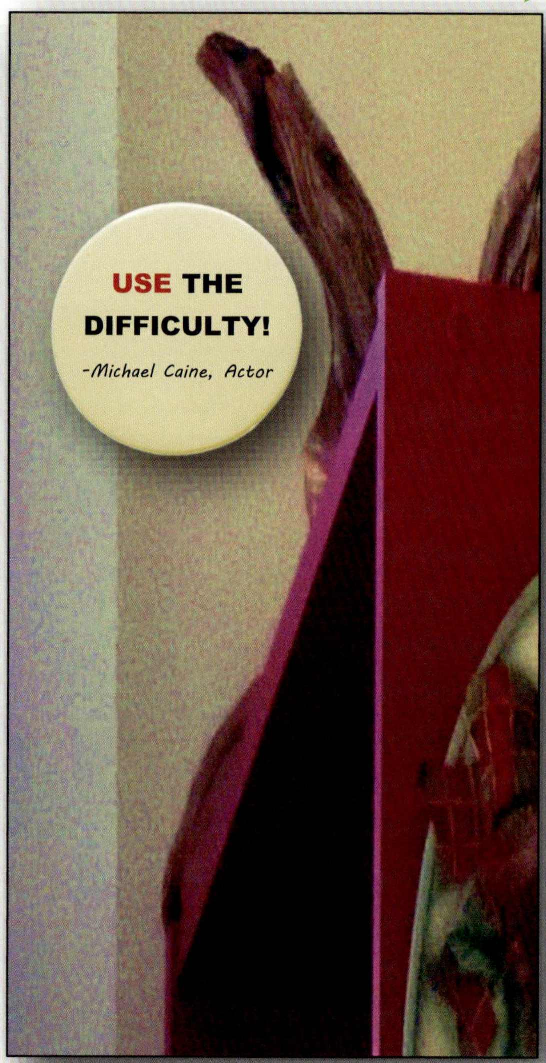

BOOTS & DINO

I want to bring a pillow camping in the California redwoods but the little country store where I shop has none. Off in the corner, I see a pile of cuddly toys and zero in on a green dinosaur that will do just fine as a substitute. That night, I position the soft toy under my head for greatest comfort, only to have it nudged shamelessly away by my friend Franny's big black doggie, Boots.

Watching Boots cuddle and chomp his new friend, I think, "How can I take it away from him?"

The next year when I arrive back at camp, Boots runs up to me, jumps on my legs and disappears out an open door. Not only does he return to drop Dino at my feet, I see that he has taken great care of his little guy!

Betha hamming it up in her Illinois kitchen

A spectacular English breakfast with master home cooking by Vera in Norfolk, England

IN THE BUFF

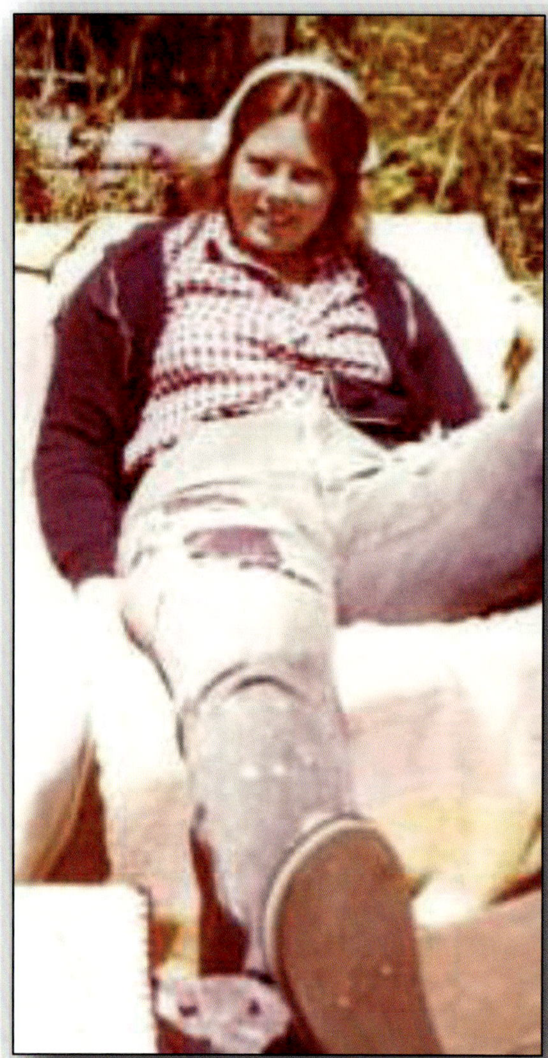

Some people like to get naked anytime, anywhere, anyplace, but not me. It isn't that I don't allow peer pressure to periodically rope me into '70s-era antics (even the quad at my college, for a time, was topless), but if I am naked and present, never think it is the real me.

Don't get me wrong, I did hang out at a nude beach or two in my day, but only because I was too wimpy to say no. I'm even featured *twice* in a Netflix movie climbing naked down a river bank, towel in hand, about to skinny dip in the Suwannee River with a bunch of Vietnam Veterans. I am also rumored to be the gorgeous woman frolicking naked in the Pacific Ocean in the same film but it wasn't me – no reason to correct anyone! I also swam naked in the Russian River in Sonoma County on land owned by ultra-conservative actor Fred McMurray of *My Three Sons* (an experience that made a woman out of me because it was there that I saw a woman with three boobs – one conical, one slingy and one shaped like a hot dog). I believe these forays into the primal world are good for my repressed Catholic girl spirit and so I sometimes push myself to show up.

On a regular basis, my roommates at the green farmhouse behind Sonoma State College parade the back forty, sunning their naked butts and feeling free as humans can feel. I have to admit my jealousy over their openness is palpable. Finally deciding that stripping naked is a skill I need to hone, I wait until everyone else is at class, gather a blanket, book, guitar, and Fritos and traipse barefoot through the tall grass to a small clearing. There, with some hesitation, I disrobe. Nirvana, right? At first, it *is* Nirvana, even when a small crop-duster plane zooms straight over me, tipping one wing. Something flying that high isn't going to bother my experiment in nakedness. He probably tips his wings at all the girls.

After taking a couple bites of corn chips, I settle into the situation like a meditation until a faint drumming sound breaks the silence. The drone is so musical (like a great bass riff on a guitar), I tap my foot to it. But as the sound grows in closeness and intensity, I have to wonder: who or what is making that noise?

Hummmmmmmmmm......or should I say Buzzzzzzzzzzzzzzzz?

I sit up, naked boobs and all, and see a line of something streaking across the brilliant blue sky. It is like someone has taken a ruler and drawn a dark line hanging in the air until it widens into a full-fledged rectangle. And then I remember – across the road, at the foothills of the Sonoma Hills – there is a farm that raises many things, including bees. Bees? Yikes!

The line-turned-rectangle in the sky now looks like the roof of our house has flown off the walls and is traveling very quickly in my direction. With no time to run for cover, I am about to be overrun literally by thousands of bees. Who knows what the newspaper will say about the naked hippy wannabe girl they find near Petaluma Hill Road, covered in bee stings, fingers bright orange from Fritos, her body frozen dead on a blanket in the back forty of a random farmhouse that is no longer there?

IN THE BUFF

Too late for any kind of defense, I flatten myself against the cool ground, stare straight up, and think of England! In seconds, the bees are over me, maybe 6 feet in the air, humming happily and headed, it seems, to the galvanized roof of an abandoned barn further on. Keeping a decent distance from the terrified human on the blanket below, they gently pass over me in a formation as intricate and organized as the Blue Angels.

In about 3 minutes it's all over, with the exception of a few strays who, like me, have trouble finding the way.

Have I just dodged a million bullets or witnessed the beauty and magnificence of nature itself?

Or both?

Since then, I have tried this exercise in nakedness multiple times, including in a hotel swimming pool in Cairns, Australia, where it prompted a very large flock of disturbed fruit bats to scream, exit *en masse* from a tree, and wake up hotel security.

To date, I have never had a successful experience getting naked in groups, although most of my friends seem pretty comfortable with the whole thing.

Maybe there are a few memos I just didn't get in life? Maybe 9 years of Catholic school has something to do with it? Seems unfair to blame the nuns. From what I know now, I bet they get naked all the time!

Canine brothers Paco, Patches & (Pepper) Jax

Franny & Robin

"DAMN, I FORGOT THE CHAINSAW!"

My name is Burton, I am a redneck
All my friends, they call me "Burt"
"Hi Burt!"
All my family from down in Texas
Make a living digging dirt.

This night in the redwoods above the Russian River starts simply enough. Our friends, *The Bad Ass Boots* band out of Oakland, are not only camping with us up on Franny B's mountain, they are also headlining the Main Street Bistro in Guerneville tonight. Halfway to the venue, Franny makes a tiny, little, almost ignored comment barely noticed by the city kids in the car:

"Damn, I forgot the chainsaw!"

Ignoring the significance of this, all I can think about (given that I flew from Minnesota to hear the band) is getting a good seat up front. Done! Once again, the *Boots* – two Billies, Joyce, Pat and Shazam – don't disappoint. It's difficult to put into words how the music of a really great band makes me feel. Moved? Joyful? Enhanced? Connected?

Packing up a five-piece band after a gig takes direction and skill that is not innate. So, around midnight three of us – Franny, Nina and me – head for my car. Somewhere up the mountain, as the driver, I make my own little exclamation that isn't ignored by anybody:

"Damn, there's a big tree blocking the road!"

"My point exactly!" Franny says, referring back to her earlier outcry. "We'll have to walk to Jill's and borrow a chainsaw."

Franny may be in her 70s, but she is an experienced mountain woman. Still, it's hard not to wonder: How the heck will she or anyone else find Jill's place in the dark, let alone locate Jill's chainsaw, with only a tiny flashlight to guide them?

"Where's Jill's house?" I ask no one in particular. In daylight, I could maybe find it. But in these conditions, I wouldn't know where to start.

"No clue," Nina shouts into the darkness. "Turn off your headlights, Diane. You'll run out of gas."

"DAMN, I FORGOT THE CHAINSAW!"

Is that a good idea? I know for a fact that there are at least two other cars eventually coming up the road behind us. But there's an even more urgent reason to keep things illuminated for me: Sitting behind the wheel of a car on a lonely, mostly unpopulated mountain where you can't see the hand in front of you (as they say) is not my cup of tea. I even sleep with the lights on in the city!

But Nina is an award-winning dancer, fast on her feet, and her day job is to supervise the maintenance teams on five Bay Area bridges. If Nina tells you to turn off the lights on your car, you turn off the lights. So here I sit, scared to death in total darkness, with the car as locked as I can get it, and Franny and Nina hiking off into near total blackness. A few chilling moments later (maybe six), I hear voices coming from the ridge to my right. Voices? Who can that be?

I lower the passenger window and brave calling out in the direction of the sounds. No one answers. Who could be walking and talking together in remote woods at this hour of the night? It's got to be 1 AM.

Freddy and Chucky, that's who!

Another wave of fear grips me, along with a terrible desire to turn on the lights even if it means facing Nina's wrath. I start up the car and about fifteen minutes later (way too soon for Franny and Nina to return), two ghostly figures approach my lit headlights carrying tools with teeth. Not very shy ghosts, they both strip to the waist in my headlights, take up chainsaws with boobs swinging freely in the hot night, and cut that sucker tree down to size. Hauling the pieces to the side of the road, Franny and Nina pop their shirts back on, bang their fists on the hood of the car, and somehow get me to let them in.

"Next time, remember the chainsaw," Franny says to no one in particular.

"Next time, turn off your frigging headlights!" Nina says to me.

"Next time," Pat, the *Boots'* lead guitarist says after pulling his van up behind us on the newly opened road, "put these women on the cover of AARP!"

P.S. After a short twist through the forest, Jill's driveway just happens to parallel the road where we were stuck. It was Franny and Nina's voices I heard as they walked together in the dark black woods.

"Took us less than thirty minutes," Franny says later. "We had this!"

Bad Ass Boots bass player
Billie D helping out the next day

I'd rather
be excluded
for who I
include
than be
included
for who I
exclude.

Nina

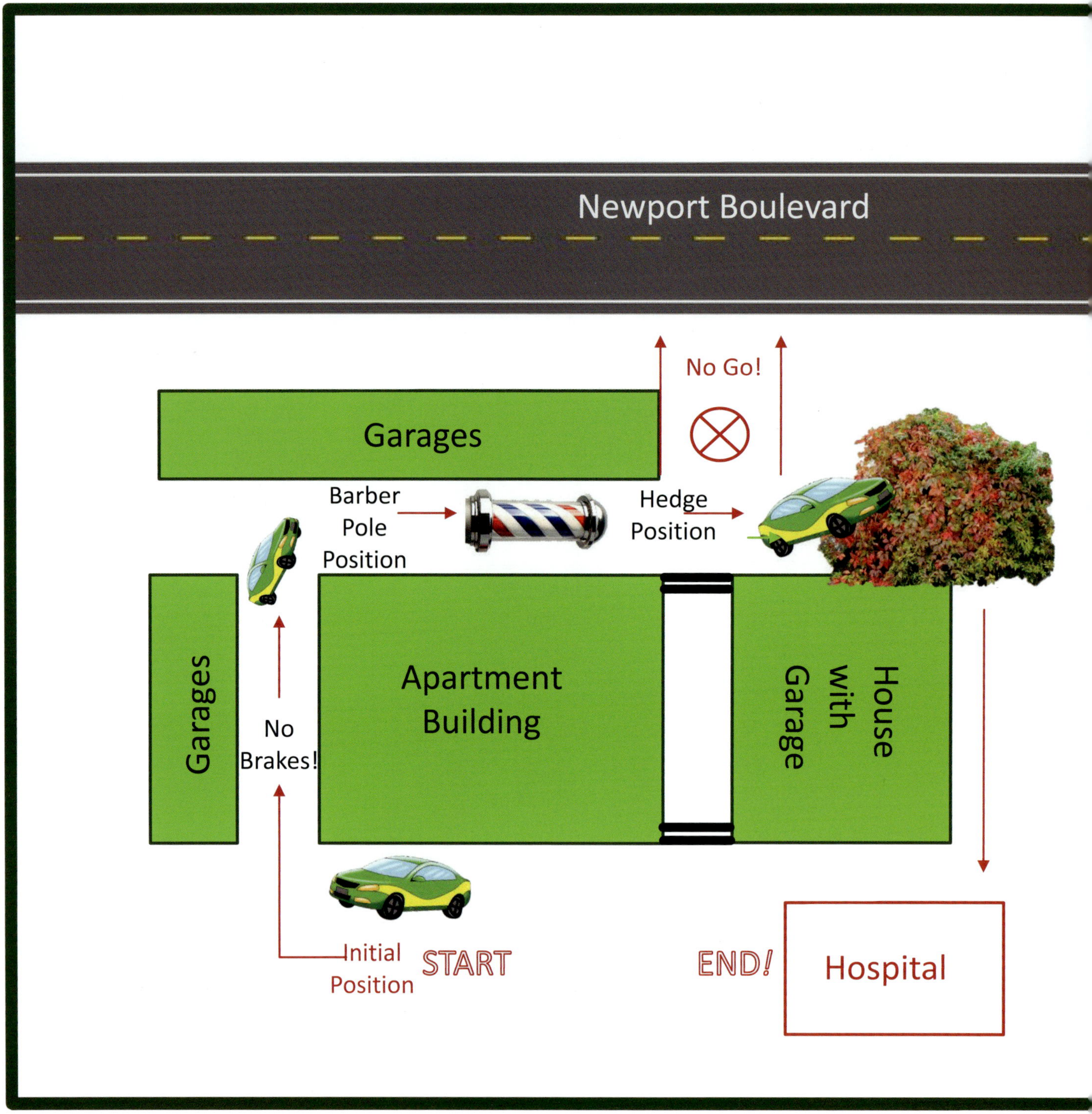
Newport Boulevard
No Go!
Garages
Barber
Pole
Position
Hedge
Position
Garages
No
Brakes!
Apartment
Building
House
with
Garage
Initial
Position
START
END!
Hospital

THE BARBER POLE

It is a morning of colors in my brand new Costa Mesa, California, studio apartment. Dressed in my uniform of navy blue shorts, white blouse and a red windbreaker jacket for my first day of work at the Huntington Beach Recreation Department, I look for all the world like a very patriotic barber pole. Aiming my green and white 1956 Ford Fairlane sedan around the first corner of my apartment building, it makes sounds I've never heard a vehicle make before. Chirping like a frog, it refuses to respond to my foot on the brake pedal!

What does *that* mean?

Rounding the corner at maybe 10 miles per hour, I am on my own. To be fair, I am young and have never heard of brake fluid before. No brake fluid equals no brakes. Like in any action movie, options are limited. I can:

1) Continue driving behind the building, down a short, steep hill and hit a house or garage;
2) Drive a few feet, turn left and end up in the middle of rush hour traffic on Newport Boulevard;
3) Pull the emergency brake to see if my head can reach all the way to the windshield; or
4) Jump.

Opting for number 4, I throw open the door and, with typical youthful abandon, hit the pavement rolling, *really* looking like a barber's pole now in my recreation leader outfit. When the motion finally stops, I attempt to stand, happy that I still can. Gathering my somewhat bloody dignity, I follow the path of my car's trajectory along the alley and down the hill where I find it lodged in a hedge, the front wheels still spinning. And then, I pass out. When I awake a short time later, I am at an area hospital with a kindly nurse offering me a bowl of ice cream.

For some reason, over the next few weeks, I get a flurry of checks in the mail from the insurance company that I used to pay tuition for the next two semesters. I never figure out why they were sending me checks but a thought did cross my mind: "Ice cream and checks might be the wrong message to send a young driver like me. But hey, bring it on!"

RUNNING OUT OF GAS

It is one of those post-divorce weeks when we are all lucky to end up fully dressed and shod. Driving east along the main road to Spring Valley High School in Wisconsin, my teenage daughter, "Susie," points casually to the dashboard.

"E means Empty" she says, having just learned little tidbits like that in Driver's Ed.

"I never forget to fill up," I tell her (ignoring the flashing red light on the gauge) knowing that this is probably a complete fib.

"Two-finger focus, Mom," she admonishes. "I repeat – E means Empty and I don't feel like walking the rest of the way to Science Club!"

Rifling through the index cards in my brain, I try to find one labeled "Last time I filled the tank," but nothing comes up.

"Heck, honey," I say. "You might be right!"

"Dah," she answers, as I hunt for an updated brain card in my head labeled "balance in my account." I have the money, luckily – but do we have the time? We are a straight shot to Huppert's BP gas station (and two miles from home), but the car is already sputtering. I am about to give up when I pull myself together, point the car straight ahead and commit to make a run for it.

"We can do this," I tell my son "Fred" who has been deathly silent in the back seat this whole time. "Hold on to your hat."

"I don't wear hats," he says with typical high school sarcasm. "And neither do you."

And on that positive note, I assess road conditions, hit the gas and make a run for the crest of the hill about one-quarter mile away. If we can get that far, we can coast down to the gas station at the bottom of the hill. Already two other cars are creeping up behind us in that weaving motion in the rear view mirror that implies "I demand to pass." But we haven't even cleared the hill yet.
"Come on, boy," I urge my vintage Toyota Corolla that will soon become a

Harry Potter art car. "If I can handle a divorce, I can handle you!"

At this point we are all yelling "You're crazy," including me. But risking a sideways glance I think I see just a touch of admiration in Susie's eyes between screams. Just seconds before we reach the crest of the hill, I actually begin to believe we might not make it. Problem is, the car has completely died. Are we about to lose all power? Will the brakes and steering wheel lock up?

Should we jump?

By now, we are fully committed, so I plant my hands more firmly at 10 and 2 (I took Driver's Ed, too) and inch the car over the crest. Soon, we are moving so fast down the hill I have to ride the brakes to keep from losing control. Nothing stops, nothing locks – we just fly. As we come closer and closer to paralleling the gas station, I remember that there are two entrances and we have just flown past the first one. But worse, even if we *do* make the second entrance, it will require a precise and swift U-turn, expert steering and a clear path to the pump to work out – and right now, there is a red Ford F-150 gassing up there.

"That's okay," I say out loud. "If we miss it, we will at least already be at the gas station and I'm sure the Hupperts will lend us a gas can."

But in the time it takes to say these words, the F-150 truck clears the pump and there is nothing between my Toyota Corolla and the blood of Jesus gas pump. Coming in a little fast, I parallel it, slam on the brakes, step out of the car, open the gas tank cover, slide the hose in, and pump $25 of Unleaded Regular into the tank. Fred rolls down the back seat window begging cash for a Subway sandwich as Susie picks herself up off the floor.

"You've got it," I answer Fred. "Cold cut combos all around!"

"Are you kidding me? My sister is a vegetarian and I'm vegan, in case you didn't notice," Fred says.

He's right. I always forget that, too.

DESIGNER DEATH

Dealing with death has undergone a revolution that some of us are just discovering. And crazy as it may sound, there may even be some humor in it.

At the risk of sounding flip and maybe even callous, I've dubbed the concept *Designer Death*. Everyone, it seems, particularly in places like California where tradition has never been a priority, wants it done their way. If Aunt Daisy wants to be cremated and have her ashes spread over Pasadena, who's to argue?

All potential Aunt Daisies listen: I'm glad you feel so strongly about your hometown – but did you ever consider who will do the spreading? More than one well-intentioned spreader has rented an airplane, opened the window, and tossed out the ashes – only to have them blow back in.

Thanks to our younger sister Kelly, my family, long-time residents of California, are lucky. It seems that our Dad's last request – to be tossed into the wind over his favorite Palm Springs golf course instead of buried – is unacceptable to her.

Kelly Jane & Dad

"I want a place where I can visit Dad in the future – and it's not going to be the 17th hole," she argues.

In support of Kelly's position is the East Coast contingent of the Ford clan, including Dad's aging mother, Grandma Margaret. They want no less than for William A. Ford, Jr. – the first Ford to die in 53 years – to be buried in the family plot. They remind the decision-makers (Dad's six children) that golf course-spreading is illegal. After a few conference calls, we all agree that burying

Dad's ashes is not as permanent as burying the whole person. We can always dig him up after Grandma dies and spread

his ashes in Palm Springs. If it would provide her any solace, we will gladly hand him over now. But this creates another problem — how to do that? Peggy, our mother, has long deferred, filing Dad's phone number under "B" for "Bozo." And although she declines attendance at the *Memorial Spaghetti Dinner & Poker Game* we organize in his honor, Mom does manage to follow it up the next night with her own – albeit subconsciously motivated remembrance – a *Turkey Dinner*, which she warns will be "strictly buffet."

It is the day of the *Turkey Dinner* that brother Kevin picks up Dad's ashes from the Neptune Society. Knowing my mother's opinion on the matter, Kevin doesn't dare bring Dad into her condo to join the festivities. So Dad is relegated to an elegant, although impersonal fate – a spot in the trunk of Kevin's "long and low" classic gold Cadillac.

Looking back, the Society's suggestion to send Dad by United Parcel Service to Boston might not have been a bad idea. As it turns out, not one of us will even consider transporting him that way. And Kelly, strongly committed to the concept of a final resting place, has already booked the two of us on a flight back to the East Coast. The decision to hand-carry Dad to our Boston relatives gives rise to another set of "Designer" problems that none of us anticipate. As Kevin hands me Dad's ashes from the trunk of his Caddie, it is a turning point in my life. Holding open Kelly's blue pillowcase – all we can think of at the moment to put Dad in – Kevin slips the orange plastic box into the depths of it. I am shocked by the weight of the ashes, although I know Dad was a big, athletic man who once hit a homerun at Fenway Park.

Here I stand, in the parking lot of my mother's condominium complex, a mess of stars over my head, holding what is left of my father. My first thought is to ask Kelly to take him, but as luck would have it, everyone has already walked away. This is ironic because of all the people in our large family, next to Mom, my relationship with Dad is the most delicate. The next day, my mother, keen on the idea of taking us to the airport (but unhinged about delivering her most unfavored ex out of California), asks her new husband Larry to drive us all to the airport anyway.

Once onboard the plane, Kelly and I look at each other, clueless as to the most respectful place to put Dad's ashes during the flight. Avoiding the overhead luggage rack, I place him under the seat in front of me and wonder how the person sitting a few inches above him would have enjoyed the flight if he knew.

By the time we are to change planes in Chicago, Kelly and I both realize that we need something other than her pillowcase to deliver Dad to the East Coast relatives in. We comb the airport gift shops, but all we can come up with is a cloth bag adorned with the sights of

Chicago and another of Mickey Mouse.

Mercifully, the saleswoman who tries to help us find "just the right thing," never asks any questions. Seeing our distress, she finally offers us a plain white paper bag with a plastic handle that is at least discreet. Back on board, Kelly and I talk over the events of the past few days from the aisle and middle seats.

"I wish Dad didn't have to ride to the airport in the trunk," she says a little too loudly. Gripping the secret contents of the shopping bag more tightly between my feet (is it even legal to carry ashes this way?), I sneak a look at the face of the man in the window seat next to Kelly. Judging by his expression, he has heard a lot more than we realize.

It is at this very moment that the denial that has helped me through the ordeal of the last few days finally breaks – and I begin to laugh. Kelly, who has not yet cracked a smile since Dad's death, catches the spirit. And there we sit, two fatherless daughters, smiles turning to laughs, laughs turning to snorts at yet another situation we humans must surmount in our journeys.

Arriving in Boston, it is soon time to pass Dad on to his relatives. Just as I suspected, when I hand over the shopping bag, a look comes over our uncle's face that conveys "axe murderer."

It is further obvious that he didn't like our choice of carriers because by the time we arrive at the church for the funeral, Dad has been transferred to a Gloria Vanderbilt designer athletic bag.

All through the Mass, Dad sits on a pedestal in that orange box – talked over, blessed over, and smoked over – only to be packed up again into the athletic bag and whisked off to the cemetery. Once there, my uncle places the box on top of a piece of synthetic turf concealing a pile of dirt, and everyone but Kelly and I pulls away. After a moment, I break the silence by starting my rental car. And as Kelly and I begin to drive down the narrow cemetery lane, I characteristically look back. What I expect to see is anybody's guess. But what I do see slipping out from behind a tree is an unshaven, middle-aged man in gray-hooded sweats and Nikes carrying the biggest shovel I've ever seen. Kelly, too, reacts in shock to the sight of the pathetic old grave digger and his shovel, and there we are. Although we don't turn to salt, it is another moment of truth. I know that through all the tears and heartache, the sense of humor our Dad has instilled in his kids will carry us through anything.

All six of us – Carol, Billy, Kevin, Missy, Kelly and myself – never agree on much. But we unanimously believe that our ability to laugh during life's lowest moments will always remain our greatest inheritance.

Reprinted from The Monadnock Ledger. All flowers shown were grown in friends' gardens.

Rest in Peace:
William A. Ford, Jr., Dad (1931-1988)
Kevin C. Ford, Brother (1957-2020)
Peggy M. Perrine, Mom (1932-2024)
Kelly Jane Ford, Sister (1966-2024)

s Vegas Review-Journal

COTTONTAIL RANCH

Planning a fun family vacation to California, we find that airline tickets are cheaper to Las Vegas so we book there. Before dawn the first morning in Nevada, we aim our rental car due north and head out into the night. Having spent so much time getting everyone dressed and ready at home, we have no clue yet of the route or timing to California except that if we drive north to Reno and turn left at the Rockies, we can skate through Donner Pass and end up in Grass Valley to visit my friend Franny's donkeys, chickens and pigs.

Once we drive past Las Vegas, things become very, very dark in the open desert. Traveling with two grade school children, it isn't long before one of them has to pee.

"There's nothing out here, Susie," I tell her. "You should have gone at the hotel. Can you just do your thing by the side of the road? No one will see."

"Are you kidding me, Mom? *Not!* There's snakes out there! I need a REAL bathroom."

"Not happening," I shoot back. "All I see ahead is darkness."

"I see something else," my now ex-husband adds to the conversation. "It's a light – maybe a gas station about ten miles ahead?"

"Good enough," I say.

"Not," Susie counters again. "*Really*, not."

I try a different tack.

"Did you know that all the bad snakes in Nevada don't wake up until the sun comes out?"

"And what about the good ones...?"

(Having smart kids is usually a great blessing – but not every second of the day.)

Things are quiet for a while and all I can see ahead is a bright red light and a shadowy billboard nearby.

"What is this place?" I ask my ex as we pull into a somewhat lit driveway with Susie screaming up a storm that, "in the bladder department, it's now or never."

"If I'm not mistaken," my ex says. "I think this is a whorehouse."

"A – what?"

"You heard me. They're legal here."

"Well, we can't take our 7-year-old daughter into a bathroom in a whorehouse!"

"Why not?"

This sentiment hangs in the air for awhile, enhancing Susie's loud demands to get this show on the road.

"Why not?" he says again as we pull up to the front door of what looks like a dilapidated complex of mobile homes. I ponder this for a minute. How long would it take for Susie to pee, anyway? And I'd be with her.

I then make the weirdest decision of my life, concurring with my very practical ex.

As we approach the weather-worn door, an equally tired-looking blonde woman in a leather jacket addresses us. "Can I help you?" she says, looking down at a very agitated Susie.

"I have a 7-year-old here who just *has* to go to the bathroom *now.* "You know how that is? Any chance we can borrow one for a second?"

"I don't know," the lady says, looking behind her. "This has never happened before. Okay, but be quick about it. Don't wake the boss."

Not far ahead, I see a toilet behind an open door and pull our daughter inside. She is already totally enamored by the place and is taking her time. Just as I lock us in, there's a knock on the door that sends my nerves through the roof.

"Who's there?" I ask hesitantly.

"Let me in NOW!"

It seems that Fred, age 5, also has to pee and has enlisted Daddy's help. I clutch Susie (who says she is "all done") and the two of us leave Fred and Daddy to task. Seconds later, my ex returns to the car banging for me to open up. Once he's in, I start up the minivan and hit the gas.

"Aren't you going to wait for Fred?" he asks.

"What? He's not with you?"

"Nope."

"Are you kidding me? You left Fred alone in the bathroom of a house of ill repute?"

"Yeah, but I told him to keep the door locked."

This reminds me of all those fathers, some of them with advanced degrees, who are good with their kids trailing behind them like ducklings at the mall.

But worse.

Pulling back to the front of the building,

COTTONTAIL RANCH

I grab the car keys and without bothering to knock, race into the trailer, this time facing off with the blonde lady.

"You've got to get out of here!" she says with some urgency. "I think you finally woke the boss!"

Pushing past her toward the open bathroom door, I see Fred still on the toilet, delightfully studying the centerfold of a *Playboy Magazine*.

"Ah, Fred," I say to him. "Please hurry, we gotta go!"

"Almost done, Mommy," he says. "Okay, okay."

Seconds later, after rushed thank-yous at the door, Fred and I are outside standing by the locked car. Zeroing in on the black plastic fob on the car keychain, I push what I think is "unlock" and miss the mark by half an inch – the red panic button sends out sounds and lights that will not only wake the boss and the bad snakes, but maybe the good ones, too.

Climbing into the passenger seat with Fred on my lap, I hand the keys to Daddy and start yelling: "Drive, honey! Drive!" But my ex has other plans.

"Not yet," he says. "Look at that billboard over there! No one will ever believe this story unless we get a picture of that."

"Good point," the storyteller in me answers, readying the camera. "Let's do it!"

Everyone's a traveler
You and me alike with
Different vision
Different sight
But the road is a long one
And doesn't it seem
That shortcuts always return
To the mainstream?

Seeking The World

Rolling down
MAIN STREET
in a town
where I never
did live.

FAMOUS PERSON STORY (THAILAND)

Don Bachardy

As part of working my way around the world with only $1,500 in my pocket, and a travel guitar wrapped around my neck, I end up sleeping across a row of plastic chairs at Heathrow Airport, waiting for a flight to Bangkok because I got here too late to get a B&B.

Just before this, employed as a temporary nanny, I'd had my own room in a fancy chalet in the French Alps. I'd never been to Southeast Asia (or even on a long flight) before, but conditions with the husband at the chalet had deteriorated. A quick exit to the coast (by gondola, train and ferry) seemed like the best recourse all around. For a while, I feel like Barbra Streisand in *Funny Girl* – with the wind in my hair and the world at my feet at the front of a New York tugboat. But the plastic chair situation at Heathrow Airport is miserable. I go through the boarding process in the morning, tripping over my own feet and everyone else's. I can sleep in my seat (that's the norm on long flights, I hear). But I have one problem with that: If I lose consciousness, who will fly the plane?

Earlier in the day, when crossing the choppy English Channel, I tried to keep myself from retching by perching on an upper deck. Downwind from a somewhat inebriated man, I watched in horror as he threw up big chunks of something over the railing and then peed into the wind. This was the exact moment when I learned never to stand downwind of an inebriated person. I'd already learned a similar lesson helping at a B&B in Alaska: Never scrub a toilet with your mouth open. Anyway, there is no way to tell where this story is leading and I wouldn't expect you to guess.

FAMOUS PERSON STORY (THAILAND)

As predicted, I don't sleep a wink on the flight across Asia, but I do get a kick when the pilot says we are now flying over Afghanistan. How cool! Will I ever get there myself? As descent nears, I ask the strangers in 3C and 3D where they are staying in Bangkok. On one hand, asking strangers where to stay sounds like the pragmatic thing to do when arriving in a foreign country. On the other, it also sounds like it could pave the way for the opening scene of a horror movie.

"Royal Hotel," they answer without hesitation. "If you like, you can taxi with us."

"Thank God!" I answer gratefully, hoping that they aren't serial killers and that the hotel is enough of a cheapie not to break the bank. Awake for nearly 48 hours so far, I am in danger of becoming the monster I fear out of punchiness. I'll pay anything for a good bed and a Diet Coke when we land. It's then, in line to get a room at the Royal Hotel, that I see a face I think I recognize, a nice face, with brown hair and wide swaths of gray across each temple. I never forget a face, and this man looks really familiar. Is he a neighbor, a friend of a friend, or maybe a lawyer I know in New York when I type on Wall Street? I decide to ask him. I don't know until later that my hair is standing on end and my blouse has come unbuttoned halfway to my belly button. But his response is quite gracious and for some reason, I think I know exactly what his expression means: "You are a very smart little traveler. I should look familiar to you, I am..."

"Oh my God," I say to the guy. "Are you famous?"

His smile confirms it. I am in deep social doo-doo.

"Don't mind me, sir. I'm from California and I haven't slept in 72 hours. I'm working my way around the world and I really, really need a Diet Coke."

I turn to face the front of the line, hoping not to bother him any further, but the exchange does not end there. Tapping me on the shoulder, I sheepishly turn to face him (at his request this time), but I am still not quite sure who the heck he might be.

"Well actually, I used to be your governor," he says. "And so was my father."

I figure it out!

"Jerry Brown, Linda Ronstadt's ex-lover!" I yell, having lost the ability to pretty much modulate any part of me by then. The guy traveling with Jerry Brown rolls his eyes and says, "Jesus Christ."

From here, the line to check-in moves and we are both saved from more exchanges.

"He is kind of nice," I think to myself. "We bonded."

The other good news is that my room is only $15/night and that the front desk has promised to send two Diet Cokes my way, right away! On the bed for less than seven minutes, there's a knock on my door with a big surprise. A smiling young Thai woman with a monkey wrapped around her neck presents a tray holding two bottles of Coke and one big pitcher of ice.

"I can die now," I say to the lady. "And I probably will."

She smiles back in typical gracious Thai hospitality and leaves me alone with my obsessions. For the next few days, as I try to pull myself together from lack of sleep, I watch Jerry down at the swimming pool with friends. Hoping to come back to earth before he leaves, I practice my entire Linda Ronstadt repertoire on my travel guitar, planning to serenade him down at the pool when I am recovered.

I miss him by a day (not sure if that's a good thing or a bad thing), and later see him on the cover of *Time* or *Newsweek* with the headline that he is currently traveling across Southeast Asia on a peace mission.

We had our time.

CHARLES & DI (AUSTRALIA)

Tripping out of a Darwin, Australia youth hostel one morning, I see a straggly crowd of locals half lining the streets on both sides. Not having heard anything about this at breakfast a few minutes ago, I wonder what's up.

"Charles and Diana are coming," one bystander informs me. "In fact, here they are."

Always up for famous people sightings, I secure a choice spot on the curb as a parade of black cars creeps slowly toward me. Inches from my eyes, the first passing car must be security; no one famous in there. But a few cars down the line, I hit pay dirt. Eyeball to eyeball with Prince Charles, it is very nice to see the future king of England up close and personal. But what I really want is a better glimpse of his wife! Bending at the waist, I innocently stare past Charles (or put another way – look right past him) to see what Diana is wearing. But Charles will have none of it. Shooting me an upward glance, he blocks my view of Diana and mouths words that I swear translate to: "What do you think I am, chopped liver?"

If it isn't for the forward motion of the car, I think Charles and I might stay locked in this dynamic forever. It is clear: Neither of us is going to back down.

And there you have it. Months or years before the world becomes aware of it, my bonny Prince Charles moment confirms that (based on his own actions and vibes), the future King of England is already feeling a bit upstaged and outdone by his amazing wife!

ON BEING A NANNY (FRANCE)

I never had a farm in Africa but I was once a nanny in France. Working my way around the world, I'd hunted for short-term, fill-in jobs – and this one was choice! Starting in Hornchurch, England, a suburb of London, I worked for a real estate developer's family whose business was to buy old houses, knock them down and build two new ones in their places.

Upon hiring me, the family is set to leave on a ski vacation to the continent with me in tow. The goal is to eat our way across France at a list of carefully chosen Michelin-starred restaurants (but only at lunchtime when the price tag is less and the kids' antics – a boy and a girl, ages 6 and 3 – will not get us kicked out).

After a tumultuous ferry ride across the English Channel, the road trip is a dream. As the father focuses on learning the various features of his new-fangled Toyota Space Camper minivan, the rest of us are free to sing songs and enjoy yummy snacks in the back. Upon stopping, we are treated to world-class cuisine in restaurants nestled throughout the magnificent French countryside.

But things change when we reach our ultimate destination – a ski chalet in the French Alps. Along the way to Courchevel, the kids come down with severe colds, ruining the father's vision of a healthy family skiing vacation there. After that, we all walk on eggshells.

But on Christmas Eve, the father's mood softens and he offers the use of his beloved minivan to me and some of the other young multinational chalet maids and butlers.

"Go out and have a good time," he tells us. "Come back whenever you want."

Within an hour, seven of us dressed mostly to the nines, pile into the van and head for the town center with me at the wheel. It is the first time I have been at a French nightclub and I am impressed by the number of tiny black dresses and the level of sophistication of the French people. Wearing a gauze dress that promised not to wrinkle in a backpack, I am way out of my league and know it. But the people-watching is fantastic.

After visiting a few fancy clubs, it is near 3 AM and time to head back to our posts. As I drive the group along the narrow city roads in light snow (very slowly, having had a drink or two myself), I really have no idea where we are and no one else does either.

"Pull over!" one guy yells suddenly. "Now!"

Have I inadvertently hit one of Santa's reindeer (the French contingent?) So far, there has been no gut-wrenching bump but the next few minutes are a blur.

"Pull over!" he repeats.

From what I can see from the driver's seat, everyone in the back has jumped out like there's snakes in the car or, in this case, something colder like polar bears. Others reach back into the van and lay the passenger seats flat; this concerns me most.

"What's going on?" I cry in English, fully aware that I am driving my boss's cherished Space Camper and speaking to compadres that know little English.

And then I figure it out.

"Oh, please don't do that!" I yell back to everyone. "Is this some kind of obscure European tradition?"

If I wasn't cool in the nightclubs, I am definitely losing even more "coolness" ground now. Having a grand old time, one butler grabs a fully decorated Christmas tree from the front of a restaurant and slides it into the van until the angel on top rests on my right shoulder.

"Get that thing out of here!" I yell, "Come on, please!"

By now, everyone is back in the car,

sitting this way and that on top of each other. Slamming the doors shut, they shout: "Go! Go! Go!" at me like a mob at a sporting event with an urgency that makes me sit taller in my seat.

And so, I move forward, fast but not too fast, straight ahead but not too straight ahead, basically onward and upward, hopefully out of harm's way. But there is an innate problem with our trajectory that none of us anticipate because we are all from far away: the restaurant is located on a cul-de-sac.

As the crowd watches us head straight into a dead end, they gather forces in front of the restaurant and step out into the street to confront us. We have no choice but to retrace our steps and now it's become "them and us." Hanging a "huey," I creep back toward the top of the street and, with great humility, mouth "I'm sorry!" at the growing crowd outside our windows. When we reach the actual spot where the tree once stood, the crowd is at its thickest and I have to stop the car to avoid hitting anyone.

"Lock the doors and windows!" one chalet maid screams at me in Spanish, a language I know something about from growing up in California. "They are trying to get in!"

As I struggle to operate the controls, the crowd starts beating on the sides and fenders of the minivan like a scene in a horror movie. Out of options, hoping everyone outside the van is sober enough to get out of the way, I inch forward.

Eventually, we ditch the tree and find our way up to our chalets with everyone but me laughing and gesturing to each other because, for the most part, none of us can speak each other's languages.

Home safe, I park and lock the car and run up to our chalet and fall fast asleep in my clothes on my bed – without doing any kind of damage survey to the van. The next morning, as I dream about people beating on my head, I wake to find that someone is *actually* beating on the door.

"Come with me," the father says as I follow him outside in last night's clothes.

"I want to show you something."

Uh-oh.

The back hatch to the minivan is open and, peering inside, I see an array of Christmas ornaments, tinsel and glitter stretching all the way along the van bed from where we stand to the front seat.

"What happened here?" the father wants to know.

"Not quite sure." I answer. (I may be uncool but I'm not a rat.)

"Not quite sure, huh?"

"Correct."

"Pack your things, girl, you are out of here! I'll let the children know after you're gone."

One good thing about backpacking is that it's hard to make the packing process take longer than two minutes. Slipping out a side door, I don't even ask for (or think to ask for) my pay. What's the point, really? I fudged up.

Making my way down the mountain, across the fertile valleys of France, over the sea to England and onto the train to Heathrow Airport, I have to admit that of all my travel stories so far (at least in terms of adrenaline and the price I paid to have them), this one is near the top of the list!

My children
"Fred & Susie"
at Stonehenge

Andrew's Family in Orkney Islands

ANDREW (ORKNEY ISLANDS)

Many years ago, in the month of October, after serving as a nanny in London, I embark on a quest to visit the Orkney, Shetland and Faroe Islands, all located above Scotland. Turns out it is too late in the year to get beyond the Orkneys by ferry. And my first train breaks down in the Highlands, which of course I don't mind a bit. It is just another opportunity for adventure. Herded on to buses, I share a seat with 15-year-old Andrew who is headed home to the Orkneys along with what I presume is a group of school kids. (What is it they say about assumptions?) Andy is curious and talkative, and early on he asks me where I'll be staying. As a "card-carrying" backpack traveler, I haven't thought that far ahead. "It isn't because I am short-sighted, fearless or courageous in the face of the unknown," I tell him. "I have plenty of anxieties. In fact, nervousness probably steals 25% of the joy of travel for me. But that leaves 75% left over to celebrate, right?"

I go on to say that when working your way around the world as I am doing, living in the now is often the best course of action. You've got to stay loose and keep dancing – or, put another way: If you get freaked out by obstacles, no one

will come near you. But if you stay calm and have faith that things will work out, people help.

As we approach the ferry to Andrew's island, South Ronaldsay, Andy offers me a bed at his parents' house and I immediately accept. As his parents drive us across the island, my appreciation for Andrew's invitation grows stronger. Driving past old-styled thatched haystacks, remnants of scuttled ships and prehistoric villages, chapels and causeways built by devout Italian prisoners in World War II, I can't believe my luck to have locals like Andrew's family narrate what I am seeing. During my time with the family, we visit many of these sites in person in the family car.

One question that is on my mind (and that I keep forgetting to ask Andrew) is: Who were all those people on the train with you, anyway?

"It was a youth church thing," he says. "We're Jehovah's Witnesses."

Oh no!

The room goes silent, but especially me. (That doesn't happen often.) All I know about his religion is *The Watchtower* newsletter and complaints about well-dressed youth knocking on people's doors to talk about Jesus when the water is boiling and the kids are sticking their fingers in electrical sockets. Remembering my "stay calm and have faith," philosophy, I try to hold back but pretty soon I hear myself saying: "Am I in trouble? Are you going to try and convert me?"

"Heck no," Andrew says. "So few people visit us here, we just want to enjoy your company. I promise we won't do anything like that. There's lots of other things to explore around here, too."

However, the congregation regularly meets in Andrew's family's home and, on the designated weekday, here I am, squarely seated in the heart of the beast. Is it safe to eat the cookies? Will there be exorcisms and dragons? Flaming red devils with pitchforks trying to penetrate my head and beat off my evil ways with Holy Bibles?

I see none of that. All I witness are sensible scripture readings followed by passionate, open discussions. Nothing weird happens, not one person wears a tie or a suit. No one tries to convert me. Actually, it seems like a nice group of people who just want to gather for fellowship and open discussion about their faith – like any other religion in the world.

Hanging with Andrew's family does not change my religion, but it does send me down another road I never expected when Andrew's father suggests I visit his neighbor Ronnie who lives by the sea.

"He's found some lovely things on his land you might find interesting. He started his own little museum."

Following Andrew's father's direction, I embark on an amazing solo walk through backroads and green pastures, finding myself at a white farmhouse with a glassed-in porch. When I knock on the door, Ronnie himself answers and I explain that Andrew's family has sent me but that I don't quite know what I am here to see. But if he has time to show me whatever it is, I'd be appreciative!

"Lovely," Ronnie says, going with the program. "I need to feed the sheep. Slip into these wellies to save your shoes. It's muddy in the fields; I wouldn't want you to get stuck!"

Wandering past herds of grazing sheep, Ronnie points out mounds of land in the near distance that he says might contain ancient artifacts and burials.

"I was taking a breather over there a few years ago," he says, "and my hand touched something in the grass that turned out to be little pieces of polished rock over 5,000 years old!"

Tomb of the Eagles by John W. Hedges

Reaching into his pocket, Ronnie pulls out four items and places them in my hand. These little bits of history have become so much a part of Ronnie's daily life, he stores them (like loose change and a pen knife) in the pocket of his jeans. They are all made of stone, smooth all right, of various colors and pleasing to the eye. But the ones I remember most are a tiny onyx button and what looks like a speckled pipe. Both have perfectly bored holes in their centers.

"Thousands of years old, you say? In my hand?"

"Oh yes," he says. "5,000 at least, I've been told."

In all my visits to museums around the world, no one has ever handed me something so old. You'd almost have to work for a museum to have this experience, I think. And then, I wonder, is Ronnie named after this island (South Ronaldsay) or is the island named after Ronnie?

And the tour hasn't even started yet!

Getting right to the point, Ronnie leads me to the edge of a cliff where he shows me what looks like the entrance to a cave. Inside, organized into well-thought out piles, were human skulls and bones (about 16,000 in total, Ronnie guesses), mixed with the talons and bones from up to 20 eagles and other birds. These avian relics are why Ronnie named the place *Tomb of the Eagles.*

Somehow I sense this is a holy place, a place no one would want to disturb. So, I stay as reverent as visiting a cathedral or a cemetery, keeping my hands to myself and simply look around.

The location is well chosen by the ancient people; you couldn't get a more scenic or serene vista built into the cliff like this. However, some of the things that happened here over 5,000 years ago might not have been as peace-loving as they appear.

Having seen the main event, we walk back to the house and I can't help but ask Ronnie more questions: "How are you going to protect all of this? Will you just leave it here undisturbed?"

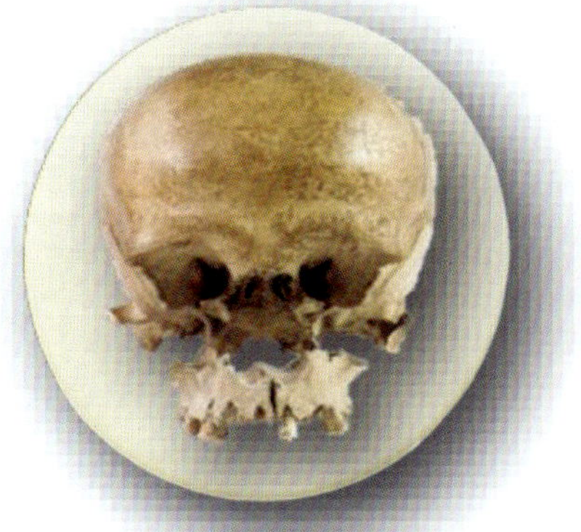

"Charlie-Girl," *Tomb of the Eagles* by John W. Hedges

"Well, mostly," he says. "I've already donated some items to the museum in Stromness. And I will send more."

As we arrive at the glassed-in porch on the side of his house, passing more flocks of sheep that Ronnie also tends as we go, he tells me that this has become his own personal museum. He hands me a coffee-colored object that looks a lot like a skull.

"This is Charlie-Girl," he says. "She's also 5,000 years old. And I've got her partner Jock over here, too. You can hold him in your other hand, if you want."

Are you kidding me? Here I am, little Diane from Huntington Beach, California, who really knows nothing of this world, holding the skull of a human being who lived on or near this land five millennia ago at the edge of the sea?

Like Ronnie, I am in the right place at the right time in history for this experience. For him to personally show me Charlie-Girl and Jock, and the wonders he found on his own land, is beyond anything I could have expected. Soon, this place – *The Tomb of the Eagles* – will become a known public treasure, open to all the citizens of the world.

Back at Andrew's house, I thank his father profusely, not only for the opportunity to visit Ronnie and *The Tomb of the Eagles,* but also for the chance to get to know Andrew and his clan. Thanks to the kindness of these families on South Ronaldsay, this visit not only connects me to the history of the Orkney Islands, but also more deeply to the history of humanity itself.

This is not the last time I will visit (or attempt to visit) *The Tomb of the Eagles.* But coming back will take many, many years.

Andrew & Esther

ANDREW (ORKNEY ISLANDS) – AND ESTHER

No one is answering!

Knocking on the door of the Jehovah's Witnesses Church in Kirkwall, Orkney Islands, I find myself still holding on to the dream of visiting the Orkney, Shetland and Faroe Islands, in that order. Almost four decades after visiting Andrew's family on the Orkneys, I find myself back on South Ronaldsay from Minnesota. My husband (my rock), who can't always believe the crazy adventures I drag him into, doesn't believe this one either. Is it possible, so many years later, to find someone who knows Andrew's family and can reconnect us? Would Andrew remember the American girl with the guitar who brushed her teeth in river water by mistake because she couldn't figure out the spigots?

Finally, someone hears my knocks.

"Is there any chance you would remember Andrew's family from out by *Tomb of the Eagles*?" I ask the kind woman as I stand outside the door on the steps of the church.

"I'm not sure. We have lots of Andrews in

Andrew & Sons

our congregation," she answers. "His surname is...?"

What the heck was it?

Somehow a name rises up within a memory that, these days, often confuses the words "umbrella" and "elevator." Even so, will this lady trust a stranger like me enough to provide any information?

The last name I remember as Andrew's is correct! I ask if she has a phone number she could call to see if anyone in Andrew's family might be interested in a short visit from us. She makes the call

ANDREW (ORKNEY ISLANDS) – AND ESTHER

Daughter Hannah

and reaches – get this – Andrew's wife Esther! (Somehow, when I travel, the people I meet are frozen in time and it's always a bit of a shock to come up to date.) Of course Andrew is married! He is probably even a father! And, Esther confirms, he remembers me. After some back and forth, Esther suggests we come by the family home and gives permission for the lady at the church to provide directions.

We've done it!

When we arrive in a driveway located not far from his parents' house, we are surrounded by lively, curious children (3 of 5) and a delightfully musical Andrew who has now aged from 15 to 51. By the time we leave, we've shared Chinese food, art projects, family histories and wonderful tidbits about the Orkney Islands themselves. We also spend time upstairs in the family room playing and singing music with my husband Jim Bob on guitar, Andrew and Esther singing solos and the kids harmonizing along. It is never hard to find songs in common when traveling – all over the world people know American songs – and they usually add some from their own culture as well.

These days, we are blessed to be online friends with Andrew's family. Our knowledge and appreciation of their homeland increases daily with extraordinary posts of wildlife, ocean shores and people, some photographs, some original artwork not only by the children, but by Esther herself. Esther is a stunning artist and photographer and her children have also inherited these gifts. If we could, we would visit the family and the Orkney Islands every year or enjoy a visit from Andrew's family at our home in Minnesota.

And what about the *Tomb of the Eagles*? Decades ago I had taken that walk from Andrew's family's house to Ronnie's – and I don't even remember it taking that long. But when Andrew gives us directions this time, it turns out to be a 5-mile walk in each direction. We take the car!

From the time I first visited the *Tomb* to now, Ronnie has passed away and the family has erected a building where people can gather for tours. But when Covid hit in 2020, the crowds dwindled, and as of this writing, the site is closed to the public. Jim and I tried to contact Ronnie's family for a visit but they would have no idea about me. All we can do is peer over fences and take pictures of the sign out front. We do manage to stay at an adjacent Airbnb that is sweet (and features a naturally "singing" toilet) but even the first-class restaurant now built on the side of the cliff there has shuttered its doors. Maybe these places will reopen in better times; maybe they already have. I am not sure if we will ever make it to Andrew and Esther's home again – or accomplish my dream of visiting the Faroe Islands – but we do continue up to the Shetlands to visit the land of *The Shetlands* TV series, including playing music with the locals in the Lounge Bar and gawking at Detective Jimmy Perez's house in the town of Lerwick. *More to come!*

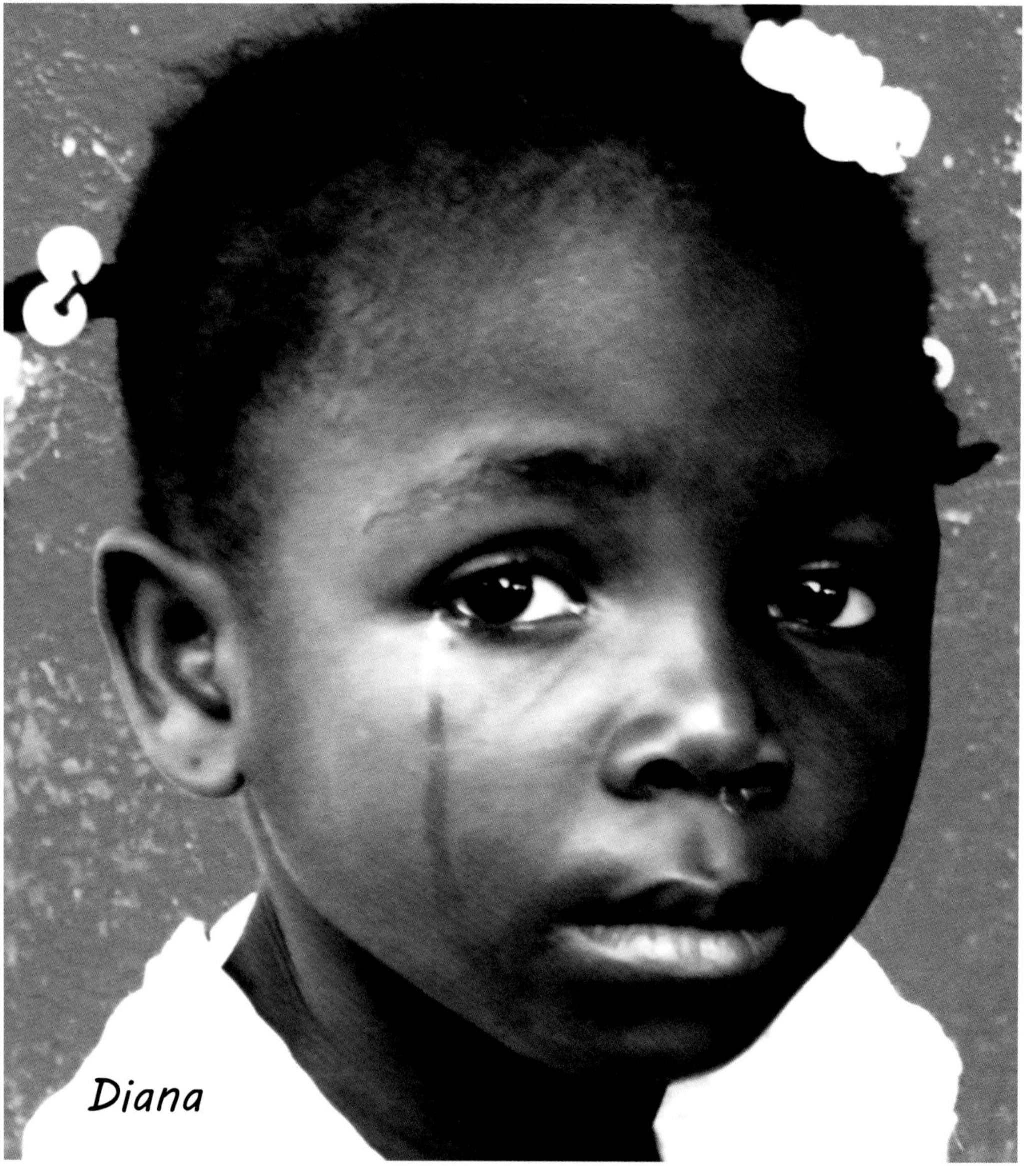
Diana

DIANA (TURKS & CAICOS)

On January 12, 2010, a 7.0-magnitude earthquake struck the island of Haiti, leaving much of the population displaced and the country in ruins.

Over Thanksgiving in 2011, I travel alone to the Turks & Caicos, an island not far from Haiti and Cuba. Known for its white sandy beaches and friendly locals, I book a room for myself on Grace Bay. My enthusiastic desire is to track down JoJo the dolphin, the marine version of Koko the Gorilla whom I've heard about from an Imax movie. Jojo was made world-famous by his frequent underwater visits to local surfer Dean Bernal. Eventually, Jojo expanded these visits to include his willing dolphin wife and two calves.

After many hours of dedicated sea gazing, I never find the elusive Jojo but I do encounter something (or someone) even more moving – a little girl named Diana.

November is a lively month in the Turks & Caicos when the locals host the famous Conch Festival. Pronounced "conk," the fair celebrates a type of mollusk that even adults like to hold close to hear ocean sounds. Hidden away in colorful, beautiful shells, the conch's meat is edible and in great local demand.

Not yet accustomed to more relaxed island ways, I flag down a "jitney" taxi to the festival grounds way too early, arriving two hours before setup. Everywhere local fishermen stretch long trails of thick fishing lines from shore to sea, ferrying catches of conch by hand to eager prep chefs in circus tents on dry land. The tents shelter tables where local cooks (like a group of nurses from the local hospital) compete for best dish awards. And for $25, anyone can buy a bracelet that allows you to sample all of the different creations they whip up. Enthralled by everything ocean (but feeling a little sorry for the entrapped conches), I stare from a bumpy dune overlooking the Atlantic Ocean wondering if I want to invest in the bracelet.

Deep in thought, as humans have been since the dawn of time near any ocean, I am gently nudged to consciousness by the arrival of a little girl, maybe 5-years-old, positioning herself next to me in the sand. Slipping her hand into mine, she stares up expectantly with starry eyes like I am her mama.

I don't say anything right away. Something tells me not to speak as she switches her gaze out to sea.

Feeling as natural as when my own children used to do the same thing, we sit there on the beach like a mother and daughter, watching the waves crash over the conch lines and contemplating our fates.

"What's your name?" I ask finally.

"Diana," she answers in English.

"Me, too! But mine is a little different; it's Diane."

"We're the same!" she says. "Look, we both have two legs! Mermaids only have one."

"True, smart girl," I say, going with the little girl flow. "Where are you from?"

Shifting her eyes seaward again, she says, "Very bad."

"Very bad? You don't like the ocean?"

Shaking her head, she just repeats, "Very bad."

Remembering that Turks & Caicos and Haiti face each other across a strait of sea, I wonder. "Could you be from Haiti, then? A refugee maybe?"

Big words for a little child. Her tiny face doesn't change expression and I think I understand the meaning behind her non-answer.

"Should we find your mama?"

Her sweet smile seems totally unconcerned about that. Grabbing my hand, she inspires me to a standing position while pointing toward the road. Up by the big tents is a food truck with a gigantic picture of a strawberry ice cream cone on the side but it doesn't look open yet. Besides, maybe her mama might not want a stranger feeding dairy products – or any products – to her little girl?

Even at this early hour, a man comes to the serving window and looks down at us.

"Strawberry, please," Diana yells up to him.

"My favorite!" he answers, "Two?"

I decide to go with it and nod.

Returning to the same spot on the beach with our treasures, we chat happily as only an adult and a 5-year-old can, pink ice cream dripping down both of our arms in the rising heat, no napkins, just a great big ocean ready to clean us when we finish. Ice creams in tummies, I feel a growing warmth on my right arm and see the little girl, who hates the ocean, asleep against me, all sticky and serene. It is one of those moments with the sparkling Atlantic in front of us and a sleeping little child next to me, that you never want to disturb.

Diana is one charismatic child. How can anyone lose track of her like this? In time, she slowly wakes with the growing festival sounds, looks up at me, and smiles sleepily.

"Let's see if we can find your family," I say.

"That's okay," she responds. "I like it here."

"Me, too, but they might be worried about you."

On a stage nearby, roadies are setting up equipment and musical instruments.

"We seem to have a lost little girl here," I call out to one of them. "Could you ask the crowd if they might know Diana?"

"Sure thing!" he says, firing up the mic and saying the little girl's name into it.

Clinging closer to me, Diana knows it is time to part. After the message is repeated twice from the stage, a spirited group of teenage girls approaches the stage and the musician points down toward Diana.

"Sister!" one girl shouts. "Naughty girl!"

There is no time for goodbyes.

Looking back, this all happened so long ago that Diana probably has her own children by now. But somewhere out there, I hope Diana is safe and warm with lots of strawberry ice cream on hand.

And JoJo the dolphin? He still regularly visits Dean Bernal who continues to don breathing gear and dive under the blue tropical waters to play. Maybe someday I will be lucky enough to see both of them in their natural habitat.

IRISH WHISKEY (IRELAND)

Bay of Tralee

The first stop of my around-the-world adventure is Tralee, Ireland. It begins with a lady named Sheila, afraid to open the door of her B&B to me because from what she can see of my face through the peephole, I might be a "boozer."

It's been a long day. I have already gotten myself to the airport in New York City, flown to the Irish coast and picked up a train to Tralee – all before dinner! I'm not sure how many time zones that is, but Sheila is right. I am worn and haggard.

"Whooped!" I tell her. "Sleep?"

"Good enough, lass," she says kindly. "This way to your warm bed!"

Out the gate, I am a bit high maintenance, but Sheila says I have no idea what she's seen before. Requesting "Bed & Dinner" (instead of "Bed & Breakfast" because I'm not big on a morning meal), she not only accommodates me, she provides a great dinner companion in the form of her handsome bachelor brother Liam. "He likes to time his visits to our mealtimes," Sheila confides. "It's the soup!"

"How do you like Tralee?" Liam asks, joining the conversation. "When you get situated here, let me show you around. This town is crack! You might want to bring that guitar of yours up the pub with us, too," he says. "Everyone will want to hear you."

Liam's immediate charm and wit catch me off guard. It's not only how he puts words together in that uniquely Irish way, but it's his enthusiasm and love for his family (and vice versa) that piques my interest. It always amazes me when I visit other countries how, within hours, it feels like I'm already part of everything. That is, except for the grumpy old man at the Shannon train station who didn't want me to get too comfortable in his country.

IRISH WHISKEY (IRELAND)

"Don't think that just because your people come from Ireland that you are Irish. You left here lifetimes ago. You are an American. Just look at those shoes!"

My shoes? What about them?

(I ask around and am told that even before we speak, many locals can identify Americans by footwear. The clues are certain types of sandals and tennis shoes.)

A few days later, when Liam repeats his request to show me around Tralee, I purposely don't mention that my family originates from nearby counties and that Ancestry.com says that I am just shy of 100% Irish on both sides because of this.

That night, climbing into the back seat of Sheila's tiny car for my first venture to a real Irish pub, she hands me what looks like a football helmet and says, "Please put this on."

The look on her face is no-nonsense, so I comply. She's accommodated all of my weird requests so far, it's only fair that I return the favor. But as people on the side of the road stop to laugh at us, I'm thinking: "This IS hilarious! Four grown adults in bright-colored helmets stuffed inside a tiny Fiat speeding to the pub three blocks away – Why?"

"It's not just me that does this," Sheila says. "It's not as crazy as it looks."

From the driver's seat, her kindly husband, whose smiley face appears to be a permanent shade of red, provides the answer:

"I like my drink," he says as we pull into a parking space in front of the pub. "Sheila won't ride with me without head protection."

"We have children," Sheila explains. "You'll see."

Hoping to lighten the conversation as I attempt to unwedge my guitar from the back of the car, I change the subject: "I must warn you, my songs are sad."

"Oh, come now," Sheila responds. "How sad can they be?"

The moment of truth comes later in the evening when Liam encourages me to take the stage. I may not be able to claim Irish heritage (per the man at the airport), but strangely I sing a lot like the other singers, go inward like they do and even close my eyes creating an effect that almost makes me look like a blind person like they do. Not only do I sing like these Irish singers, I look like them, too. Some members of the audience are doppelgangers of my mother, father, siblings and grandparents. Maybe the man at the train station is wrong? Maybe I am Irish after all? If this was China, would I be having the same experience?

While the lyrics to the songs the others sing are traditional or jolly (even if tragic), mine are…?

As I return to the table, I can see that my assessment of my own music is not far off. Liam excuses himself for the loo and Sheila looks emotionally stricken.

"You weren't kidding!" she says, tears turning to laughter. "Your voice is magnificent but your words – Ouch!"

"I only write songs when I'm sad," I explain. "When I'm happy, I'm too busy having fun and the words don't come."

Not wanting to don the helmets again for the ride home, Liam suggests we walk back to the house. Great idea but the route he chooses is curious. Not only does he take me to the town cemetery where he introduces me to his dead wife, he also tells me that the keening I hear on the wind, along with the putrid smell, is the local abattoir where pigs get turned into bacon. I am on this trip to learn about other cultures, I remind myself. Liam is sharing some of the most important experiences of his life, personal and cultural. That's a good thing! A few minutes later, though, on the swings at the playground oddly located next to the cemetery, Liam proposes marriage, ring and all.

"Ah, jeez," I say out loud. "I can't do this, Liam. This is day number four of my around-the-world adventure and Tralee is my first stop!"

Smiling confidently at me, he seems to anticipate this. (Has he done this before?) "Let me tell you about when the train to Dingle used to run through our land," he says. "My uncle's true love has left for America and he is keen to follow her. So one night, he gathers his things and goes down to meet the train, but the train won't stop for him. So, the next night, he does this again – but this time he lays down on the tracks with a lantern. I'd lay down on the tracks for you, Diane."

Wow, this guy is good. Add the exotic Irish location, the fabulous music and the warm people and I am almost hooked. But at the moment, I think my face is reading something akin to horror.

"Okay then, dear one, is this too fast for you? How about this? Come visit my pretty house – it stretches over an entire ridge on the Bay of Tralee. Even better – you are working your way around the world, right? Why not be my housemaid for a fortnight? I can totally picture your sweet face on my land. I'll pay you to put your trip on hold for a short while until you can decide. We can ride my motorcycle through the hills and I can show you more of this part of Ireland. And if you still don't want to marry me after that, you'll have a few extra coins in your pocket to help you along the way."

As a single woman in her thirties, free to make any choices I see fit, Liam and his life as a colorful dairy farmer on the Bay of Tralee is making points. *Big points.*

The next day, before I can protest, we are all packed into the tiny Fiat again, football helmets and all, headed for the Bay of Tralee. To Sheila's point about her husband, the only stop we make between Tralee and Liam's farm is a moonshiner's shack where we are offered whiskey samples that burn a hole through my American shoes!

As we finally approach Liam's house, Sheila narrates the scene and, I have to admit, upon first impression, I am completely captivated. The whitewashed house is a rambling one-floor structure, almost like 6 or 7 houses set side by side above the bay with stunning views that stretch forever. But as we pull into the long driveway, I can't help but notice multiple windows curtained by bedsheets and three tricycles in the grass. And although I don't see any children, we do have to circumvent a pile of laundry that reaches almost to the ceiling of the foyer. Sheila looks away, leading me into the kitchen where Liam is happily drinking coffee.

"So, you made it, lass," he says, jumping up and giving me a bear hug. "That's a start!"

As with everything Liam, emotions and events come fast and furiously. Somehow I feel like I am in the middle of an extremely intriguing job interview, but I don't know what it's for.

Tricycles?

As if on cue, Sheila and her husband leave the room and Liam pushes a chair toward me. I take a seat.

"I did save a few little details to tell you when you could see things for yourself," he says. "Last year, I am sad to say, my beautiful wife died in childbirth as you know from the cemetery. But it is much more tragic than that. Using her last breaths of life, she birthed a little babe – and then died on us, died on me. Sheila is a huge help, as you can imagine, a godsend. But she can't be here all of the time and I can't oversee the farm and the children by myself. I am not looking for hired help, Diane. I want a partner with heart and energy, a wife, just like you."

So far, Liam is not only making a great case for me to end my around-the-world trip, he is unpacking my bags.

"The last baby my wife bore is good now. But at birth, she was so small she fit into the palm of my hand." He stretches out his right arm to illustrate his point and bares his palm to me. "Lizzie is our eighth child, all under the age of 10, still sickly but a fighter like her mother. Thanks to God, she lives."

And with that, Sheila returns to the room with a mob of animated children. We are now surrounded by multiple sticky fingers and delightful kid sounds. My thoughts drift somewhere between "How do I get out of this gracefully?" and wanting to jump in with both feet like Julie Andrews in *The Sound of Music*. I am honored and, like Maria in the movie, I even play the guitar! "Doe, a deer, a female deer…!"

But then, carrying the littlest baby, Sheila whispers something in my ear that is completely unexpected:

"He'll never be faithful to you, dear. For sure, there will be others."

Whoa. I am overwhelmed by the kindness of this gesture. It's not hard to put together that Sheila, the woman keeping both families going, is warning me off against her best self-interests. Later that night, I pack my bags at Sheila's and make my final plans for leaving the lovely village of Tralee and this lively and surprising family. The next morning, with something like 352 days left on my around-the-world airline pass, I slip out of the house for the train station and the Dingle Peninsula with a myriad of mixed emotions.

I do not know if I ever could have made a difference in Liam's family – maybe yes, maybe no. But more than once, as I continue my journey around the world, I think back on the faces of all those beautiful children – and wonder.

IRISH WHISKEY (3 GENERATIONS) *(Song)*

Irish whiskey, holy water, bones and bottles, babies, shelter
Hand to mouth we grew as children in the south of any city you call home
Raised by iron fists of father and the anger of our mothers
We learned the roles of parenthood any way we could
And many-a-time, that moment came too soon

> I am your son, you are my father
> And to you I must confess that I don't want a stinking inheritance
> Binding my existence to an ancestry of fools, fears and tough innocence
> Anyway you died too soon
> All I want is that silver spoon
> For the mouths of my children
> And here I am, what a sham, there's Irish whiskey in my hand
> I thought I had a choice to listen to some inner voice
> There's no common sense – just inheritance

Through my body runs your blood
Mixed with fluid of another day and other people's love
And I don't know where I'm going
Though I sure know where I've been
I've been baptized by your blood and sweat
and cleansed of all original sin
Though I still love that Irish whiskey
(with holy water on the side)
And my babies rattle bones in bottles
Under shelter of a newfound pride
In common sense – and inheritance.

Blaze

JAX

Betty

CALAMARI (ITALY)

Most people remember time spent in Venice, Italy for the historic churches, plazas and canals. My mother is not so lucky – she did misstep and slip into one of the canals in her eighties – and had to be rescued. But she was a hearty soul and brushed it off quickly. Other stories I've heard about the place stand out, too, especially one about the food. The food?

On an age 18-35 camping tour of Europe, I need one good meal cooked on a real stove for myself. Drifting off on my own to enjoy the city, a big priority is also to hone in on a good restaurant. Success – at least three locals suggest Antonio's – and here I sit at a table all by myself next to a spectacular window highlighting a bridge over a canal. Because it is 3 o'clock in the afternoon, most of the tables are empty, and it appears to be just me, one waiter and an elderly couple in the corner holding down the fort.

"I'll have the *bistek* and spaghetti," I request in English, hoping that what I order will materialize as a nice dish of pasta and a steak, given the language differences. Smiling questioningly, the

waiter nods like he *sort of* gets it, and heads into the kitchen with his notepad. I am in heaven – how can I not be? Sitting alone in a peaceful restaurant, staring out at the sights of – yikes! Something has just fallen off the ceiling or walls and hit me lightly on the forehead. Pawing it, it feels wet to the touch and I am hoping it isn't the *red* kind of liquid.

Yikes again! I get another blast of the wet stuff which luckily is not blood but some other indistinguishable color. Deciding not to make a big thing of it, I scrutinize the ceiling and walls trying to figure out the source.

Another hit! Sitting there looking like I've had a glass of dirty water thrown in my face, you'd think I would switch tables in the nearly empty restaurant.

CALAMARI (ITALY)

"This is too much."

Rising to find the waiter, I see him exiting the kitchen with a nice big plate of steaming food for me. This is a dilemma: Be quiet and enjoy a plate of real Italian pasta in Italy now, or go into the process of lodging a complaint about the restaurant's possibly leaky roof?

I take the middle ground, accepting my meal "as-is" while at the same time trying to ask in Spanish (the closest I can come to Italian) why my face is wet. Looking as puzzled as when he took my order (which unfortunately is delivered as fish rings and fries), his face lights up.

"Calamari!" he says to me with some excitement. "Calamari!"

"Yes, I know!" I answer. "Beef steak," I say pointing to the fish on my plate. "Not calamari, beef steak, please." He seems to be having a jolly old time watching the water drip down my face. I am losing patience. "Say that 'C' word one more time and I'll knock a-a-a whole dollar off your tip! Or maybe fifty cents – what's that in lire?" (The man does work hard for a living.) I used to have this same problem with my kids: "Do that thing you just did again and I'm going to – you know, take away – or you'll have to, or you won't get to – you know what I mean!"

His still gleeful demeanor gets me thinking: What *is* going on here? I ordered beef steak and got fish rings, fries, and a sponge bath. And then it hits me (the idea, not another shot of liquid) that the waiter has had it right all along! The answer to both dilemmas is the same word! It seems that my choice of dining table has placed me next to five silver buckets of, who knows, maybe four generations of water-shooting squid? And they're mad as hell and ain't going to take it anymore! Who's on my plate, anyway? Cousin Pino? Uncle John?

"Calamari!" the waiter repeats, pointing at the silver buckets and smiling at me from behind one missing tooth. *"Capiche?"*

"I get it now!" I answer, chomping on a fish ring. "Calamari, not *bifsteak*!"

GYRANDA
It rained last night. Puts everyone in a good mood at breakfast. After clean-up, I steal a quick look toward my hut and see a misty view of old bending trees, little dogs fighting over big bones, white-legged horses with children on their backs, lazy silver grain tanks, and giant squawking birds landing and taking off with wing spans the size of mine. And finally, the sun appears, struggling hard to take its usual place of power above it all. But no one wants it to. Suntans are for banana boats and rain feeds cattle. And to me, that's what it's all about at Gyranda. Diane Ford Craig
(American Cook, 1988)

GYRANDA CATTLE STATION (AUSTRALIA)

Dianne, a songwriter from New York, had seen our advertisement for a cook in the Queensland Country Life when
in Cairns and came down by bus to Theodore. She seemed ill at ease when shown her cottage. It didn't enter my
she may be worried by the darkness and the quietness of the bush at night.

We had noticed the light on in her room when we got up during the night. Next morning Dianne looked terrible
slept a wink. She wanted to leave immediately. When I asked her what was wrong, she drawled "It's the bugs",
while to figure out the problem. Dianne, not being accustomed to anything but the bright lights of New York,
terrified of the dark, so had left her light on. That had attracted all the insects from miles around. They had
her head, in her hair and crawling around her bed. To aggravate the situation all the local green frogs turned up
the bounty. Dianne was terrified and resigned on the spot!

Once we gave her the explanation, she agreed not to leave. It was SO foreign to her. To give her credit, she did
weeks we required (while Meryl was away). She had a beautiful voice and gave us nightly renditions accompan
guitar.

Weekend Muster Big Shock For Yankee Way Down Under

By Louise Joyce
Australian Correspondent

During the weeks leading up the Sydney Royal Show, things were fairly quiet on the home front. The drought continued, with no end in sight. Everyone got on with their own business, as usual.

We were busy with mustering, branding and dehorning. So busy, in fact, that work continued throughout the weekend.

At present, on "Gyranda" we have an American girl cooking for us, for a few months. Dianne Ford has spent the last 10 years in New York, and had not long arrived in Australia, before she came to Gyranda.

You can imagine the cultural shock she had, coming to a "cattle station" of 23,000 acres. She felt she had literally stepped back in time, particularly to find I was involved in teaching my own children. She was quite amazed that they tune in to "School on the Air" over a transceiver which links correspondence children throughout many thousands of square miles in Queensland, to a teacher as far away as Charleville (400 miles).

Getting back to this weekend muster! Dianne thought it would be a "fabulous experience" to join in on a muster! "A REAL LIVE MUSTER." (This being possible by the fact that she doesn't "cook" on the weekend.)

She advised us that she could ride, although hadn't for a number of years. We brought in the "right horse" (used for running the work horses in, on), saddled her up, and got Dianne mounted.

The mare, sensing that her rider was not terribly experienced, slowed down to a snail's pace...and could not be enticed to alter her stride! I loved Dianne's remark later: "This horse only has one gear! First" *and* "I wish this horse had cruise control", as she rubbed her aching legs!

During the course of the muster of cattle to the yards, I had tried to prepare Dianne for what she was about to experience i.e. expl branding and deho cedure, elaborating detail the neces merits of it.

Obviously, the thoughts had oc Burnett, so at some the muster, he likewise. Unknown several of the thought it wise Dianne be terrified of much WILD? life she countered during frogs, spiders, "bugs" (which refers sort of insect.)

By the time we the yards, Dianne ing a bit pale, in of this event she HAD ch—to prove to that she was strong she thought she was!

She stood trans the proceedings first few calves were and dehorned. A look came over her face, remarked "That's not bad as I was expecti

A case of ation!

Reprint of article by Louise Joyce (and it's all true!)

"MONOGAMY OR POLYGAMY?" (CAMEROON)

Sister Genevieve's silver anniversary with the Little Sisters of Saint Therese

The first time I attend a church service as a guest tourist of the Sisters of Saint Therese in Tiko, Cameroon, Africa, there are many surprises. The congregation is English-speaking but so rural that my presence causes a stir among the children: I am the first white person they have ever seen. Running their fingers along the skin of my arms, they marvel at our differences. I try to make a good first impression for "the team."

As the service progresses, the young priest announces the next song we will sing is from the Catholic hymn book. I know every word: *Blowing in the Wind* by Bob Dylan is right there on page 236! The surprises continue when my friend, Sister Genevieve (who I once worked with at The College of Saint Scholastica in St. Paul, Minnesota), steps up to distribute Holy Communion to the people. This is the first time I have ever seen a woman in this role although I hear it is becoming more common; I am delighted.

When staying as a guest of the nuns, church services are daily and include weddings and funerals. I attend them joyfully and respectfully as cultural experiences.

"MONOGAMY OR POLYGAMY?" (CAMEROON)

In just a day or two, there is already a substitute priest at mass because the other young pastor, I am told, has contracted encephalitis. As a tourist, I am fully inoculated for all of the various diseases I might encounter, but sadly, the people of the village who live with these illnesses on a daily basis are most often unprotected.

The next service I attend is an actual funeral. The mother of one of the town's leading citizens has died. Over tea in her daughter Lydia's living room, I ask why I see so few white-haired people in Tiko. Lydia, who is obviously younger than me, says that people just don't live that long in this part of Cameroon. Now that Lydia's mother is gone, most of the older people are my age, according to Sister Genevieve. It is an amusing oddity, then, to see me – a 65-year-old woman wearing tie-dye and stretch jeans – traveling the world by herself.

Lydia's mother's passing is mourned over the course of two funerals: one in her birth village (a 14-mile walk without a paved road) and another in town. Knowing that I could not have managed all those miles in the heat and with a recent knee injury, Lydia thoughtfully invites me to the funeral mass in town. It will be a colorful affair. Many of the ladies of Tiko, although financially challenged, dress in the most creative, colorful clothes. I tell Lydia that I might not be able to attend the funeral because all I have with me to wear (having just spent a month walking the Camino in Spain) are jeans and t-shirts.

"That is fine," Lydia says, when I finally admit this. "We will make you a dress!"

With that, she takes my hand and walks me across a dirt road to a little shack where a woman is operating an old-style Singer treadle sewing machine with her feet.

"She'll measure you now," Lydia says, giving instructions to the lady. It barely sinks in that not only is she about to make me a made-to-order dress, Lydia has asked her to use the family's specially printed fabric that will identify me as almost family at the funeral. This feels like too much fuss when it is clear that Lydia has to deal with all the preparations for a large funeral and also the passing of her dear mother.

"The funeral is in two days!" I tell her. "Please don't do anything special for me."

"Ah, but this lady is a very good seamstress," Lydia says. "She is so good that it will be ready by tomorrow – our gift to you."

I have never had a made-to-order dress before and I am intrigued. After the fitting, as we return to our seats in the living room of Lydia's fashionable home, I ask her which town her mother will actually be buried in – this one or her home village?

"Right here," she says, pointing to the floor.

"Here in the village?" I ask.

"Yes, right here," she repeats. "It's always best to keep your loved ones close in these times. There is a lot of political unrest in Cameroon."

"*How* close will you keep her then?" I repeat, sure that I misunderstood her.

"Those tiles under your feet are removable," she says. "Down there."

Never did I think that someone's mother might be buried beneath my feet while having tea with her daughter on the family coffee table above.

"Is anyone else, ah – down there already?" I ask casually.

"Everyone in the family who has died since we built this house is there," she says. "We like to make sure we know where everyone is."

What a touching thing to love your family so much that you want to keep them *that* close, I think.

At the funeral, when I walk down the aisle with the villagers in my new dress with the white piping, I feel like a blushing bride. The lady in the hut did such a perfect job; I've never worn anything so beautiful and fit to form. I appreciate being able to honor Lydia's mother in such a fine dress and in the family's special fabric.

"MONOGAMY OR POLYGAMY?" (CAMEROON)

After that, I vow to help support the seamstresses of Tiko by ordering dresses for all of my women friends back home. This project will require multiple bolts of fabric and Sister Genevieve and I go shopping in the tents and shacks of Tiko's open market. We find all kinds of fun choices like one print that depicts the various stages of a chicken's life (from the egg to a hen), not forgetting the rooster! We love the fabric so much that we have two chicken dresses made – one for each of us.

Later that year, when I marry James Craig in Minneapolis at age 65, Sister sends us a special wedding gift of yellow and turquoise outfits that we wear at our Camino-style wedding. Jim has never worn plaid pants before, but when he slings his guitar over his head to serenade our guests with his band, it all comes together. To complete the Cameroonian experience, Sister invites me to another local ritual, a triple wedding where the brides and grooms (after a thoughtful lecture on how to have a good marriage) are each required to state their marriage preference:

"Polygamy or Monogamy?" the congregation shouts in turn at each couple. Actually, this is a trick question. If anyone answers "Polygamy," the wedding is cancelled and everyone must go home according to recent laws of the land.

"Monogamy," all of the brides and grooms answer back to the crowd. And, with that answered correctly, we all move outside to celebrate the occasion.

The graceful
Sister Genevieve in
Tiko, Cameroon

THE CAMINO

The Camino Frances starts in Saint-Jean-Pied-de-Port, France, and continues for 500 miles to the cathedral honoring St. James in Santiago de Compostela, Spain. People of all ages, from all countries and all walks of life, choose to walk the Camino, or part of the Camino, for their own reasons. While it began as a Catholic pilgrimage experience, over the centuries it has expanded to include everyone.

THE CAMINO (SPAIN)

Someday, if you find yourself sitting next to a chubby old couple with big paper plates of homemade goodies at a semiannual Camino dinner, and are itching to ask them questions about:

- How far in advance to book hotels in Spain;
- How much to train in advance for "the trail;"
- If there are enough beds and bathrooms on the Camino; and
- Is it safe to walk alone (or even at all) at our ages and conditions?

We have a story for you.

Word is that the Camino begins the moment a pilgrim comes home. For Me, it started long before I stepped on the plane to Spain. After 22 years of marriage, a sad divorce, two brilliant kids, 17 good years at a soap company, and a messy move from Western Wisconsin to Saint Paul – this Camino needs to be All Mine, you know, for ME, specifically chosen to feel, heal and deal – Me! To get up every day and worry only about walking, eating and sleeping – yes! But in my case, the Universe decides to send Me an extremely ill-timed message, first in the form of excruciating knee pain. Really? What am I supposed to learn from that?

As I drag my left leg around my pre-Camino world (including, embarrassingly, the national Camino gathering in Saint Louis), life sends me yet *another* message. This time, it's a positive message in the person of a fiancé. Although Jim turns out to be a way better gift than meniscus tears and severe osteoarthritis, how can I invite him on the Camino when it is, well, already totally reserved – you know: For Me.

"Everyone walks the Camino alone," I hear people saying. Adding Jim to the mix will just mess Me up, right? But for now, from the sidelines, Jim patiently helps to solve all of my dilemmas:

- Where do we start the walk (St. Jean or Burgos)?
- What city do we fly into (Dublin, Paris or Madrid)?
- What do we pack (i.e., Is a half bar of soap better than no soap at all)?

- What about advance training? (Do I push my knees to the limit at Lake Phalen in Minnesota first; or wait and baby them until I hit the Camino in Pamplona)?

One moonless night in Saint Paul, amid all the traffic noise and gunshots, just days before my flight to Spain, I hear myself asking Jim if he wants to come on the Camino. Am I crazy? What about all the "Me" stuff?

"Sure," he answers quietly, quitting his job the next day on the way to REI to find a 2-ounce down jacket with a stuff bag, effective bed bug spray, and an infrared headlamp.

Since his flights were booked last minute – well after mine – we arrive in Pamplona on different planes three hours apart. Primping too long in the bathroom after my flight, I return to a desolate, absolutely unpeopled baggage area. Worse, Jim is supposed to have arrived first and there is no sign of him. Unlike me, his international travel history and ventures from West St. Paul beyond business are limited. He could be anywhere! Afraid to go past security because I might not get back in, I wait and wait, but no one comes. Did Jim miss his flights? At wit's end, I finally venture outside baggage claim only to find a concert in progress. It seems that everyone on security duty at the Pamplona airport have abandoned the baggage carrels and are currently harmonizing with Jim to all of his Beatles' favorites.

Jim's Camino has already begun.

But what about Mine?

No matter. We are here to walk, eat, sleep, feel the sun/rain on our faces, enjoy spectacular scenery, and interact with fascinating *peregrinos*, right?

So, that's what we do. Putting one foot in front of the other, we walk. With yesterday's underwear drying next to the symbolic scallop shells on our backs, we walk and walk, dodge bikes and Olympian-wannabes, and walk a little more, often dragging that damn leg of mine behind me. We connect with people. We sing with people. We dance with people. We cook and eat with people. We lose people and they lose us. I praise myself for choosing to walk in April instead of September because someone told me that there is less toilet paper on the sides of the roads then. But in the end, we never see one sheet!

And when we finally reach Santiago de Compostela (and claim our documents for the 125 miles we managed to walk), we return home just after my 65th birthday only to marry six months later. Any man who can patiently and kindly accommodate a too-round, limping woman barely able to achieve four miles a day has my vote. And what did we learn from walking the Camino?

1) Sock liners and knee replacements are good.
2) Have faith; the Camino will provide.
3) Pack lightly and carry two big sticks.

And, most importantly…

4) Forget over-planning. Just show up!

My First Selfie
(Santiago de Compostela, Spain)

Scary Stories

THE RUSSIAN HAT MAN

It is late at night and, fairly drunk, the mother comes home just minutes after the bars close not sure what to do with me, the babysitter.

"I can't leave the children alone, so I guess you either have to spend the night or you're on your own on the streets."

"No problem," I say, stashing the few dollars I made into the back pocket of my jeans. "There will be a taxi."

It's hard to picture Greenwich Village devoid of activity at any time of day or night, but I guess even New York City slows down sometimes. Home is just across the Village, which is good, because every taxi that passes me is full.

Halfway to my apartment building near Bleecker and Thompson Streets, I hear a "tip-tap, tip-tap," coming from the sidewalk a few car lengths back. All I see is a very non-threatening man dressed in a grey overcoat and black Russian hat looking in the other direction.

"What stalker dresses so fashionably and taps his shoes on the pavement so that everyone on the street can hear him?" I wonder.

I hesitate to take my usual route home because I don't want to show the man where I live. I'm almost 24 years old and have lived here safely for four years with no problems so far. I feel comfortable enough. And the Russian is keeping his distance, too; he doesn't look or act like a stalker at all.

Reaching my turn, I decide to take it, remembering that halfway down and across the street is an all night mom/pop grocery store where I buy little things like microwave popcorn and Diet Coke. *But not tonight.* I can take refuge there if I need it.

Sneaking a look back, I see that, like me, the man has also turned the corner. He is now, as he has been, on the same side of the street but far back. The distance he maintains is comforting, but the tapping of his shoes on the pavement Is unnerving.

"Don't get paranoid now," I say, talking myself down. "You're almost home."

But only part of me is listening – my mind and body are contemplating divorce. One denies everything while the other is already fingering the building key in my pocket.

Halfway down the block, just across the street from the grocery store, I consider crossing over. Instead, I continue the fifty paces or so to my building, wondering if I cross, will he cross?

Eventually, I do make the move – but he doesn't follow me. He stays a respectable distance back and across the street. *Whew*. This is a good thing, I figure. Carefully placing one foot in front of the other (afraid that I might stumble and tip him off to my fear), I hesitate at the entrance to the convenience store just steps from the front door of my building. I curse myself as I walk right past it.

Seriously? Why don't I stop?

Completely engulfed now in a full mind-body split, what I am seeing with my eyes is not matching my instincts. If I hide out in the store for a time, what will stop him from waiting between buildings until I come out? Waves of shame pass over me for being so paranoid. Clearly no one is following me – not the man in the Russian Hat with the taps on his shoes or the woman in the floppy hat who has just exited the market, tossed a purse into a car, and driven off. I could have said something to her, anything, but I didn't say a word. Nothing came to mind.

Why?

I am literally ten steps from home when I realize that my brain is disconnecting but deep in my pocket, my hand is stiffening around my building key.

And then my legs start running!

In freeze frame, it feels like the world around me is standing still and my body is running a marathon. No time now for false sensations, I focus on the tasks at hand.

Reaching the first door of my building (the one that anyone can open), I pull the handle and it gives – but I'm not safe yet. There are still more obstacles, including the second glass door, the one that requires the key in my pocket, the one that's always locked and protected by security buzzers in each apartment. If I fumble this (and this guy is really following me), it will take too long to recover. Jamming the key into the lock (the one that's been at the ready longer than I have), it works. I'm in!

"Close call," I think as I slam it shut, not sure any of this high emotion is actually necessary. Taking a moment to breathe that perennial sigh of relief we all feel in situations like this, I turn around to see if I can see anything unusual through the glass door.

I do. Inches from my face is the man's face – staring directly at me with only a pane of glass between us. No tapping shoes now.

Man, is he fast.

With the intimacy of a goodnight kiss, he calmly and confidently declares through the glass (backlit by street light), that I should open the door and let him in.

Is this really happening?

"Forgot my keys, Miss" he mouths politely, "Open up please. Please?"

In shock, I study his face to see if it is familiar. *Nothing.* I've never seen him before and he doesn't live in this building. He is already pressing security buttons hoping someone is stupid enough to buzz him in at this hour.

Even so, there is still another decision to make – given that my ground floor apartment is fifty feet down the long narrow hallway. If I run there now, he will see me go in. If I don't run there, I may soon be alone with a mad man in a long, empty hallway that does not contain any other apartments but mine.

Does this guy already know where I live?

I don't think so. Eyeball to eyeball, I catch his vibe. This is a crime of opportunity, I'm guessing, made possible by the closing of the bars and the lack of taxis on the streets. "And he's older than me, decades older," I think, but what difference does that make, especially if he has a weapon? *"A weapon? I hadn't thought about that!*

Choosing to make a run for it (with him watching) is an impossible choice. Do I stay, go, or assume that the locked door will hold and he will eventually go away? Staying put is not a viable option either.

I run. Taking the long hallway in jumps, I do the key thing again without hesitating, slam the door behind me and, once again, I'm in. Behind two locked doors now (but in full view of what truly is a stalker), I start giving myself orders: "Engage the deadbolt! Dial the police! Look to see if he's still out there!"

Tripping on the long cord of my old-style phone, I position myself at the peephole, looking away from it only long enough to dial 9-1-1. Unfortunately, he is still there, still pushing random buttons hoping to get in. Every few seconds, my own buzzer sounds, too. "That's bold – he thinks he can still access the building even without a key?"

"Hang up and keep the door locked," the operator tells me. "Someone will be there shortly. Don't open the door for any reason."

THE RUSSIAN HAT MAN

“Do you have to tell people that?” I ask her.

“You’d be surprised,” she answers. “People get really stupid in these situations. It’s shock, maybe.”

“What do I do if he tries to break my door down before you get here,” I ask. “What if he gets in?”

But this is New York City. The 9-1-1 lady is already on to the next emergency and—the line is dead.

Replacing the phone on the coffee table, my buzzer sounds again before I can get back to the peephole.

I freeze. Jesus! Is he still at it?

This whole cat-and-mouse game has lasted less than 2 minutes. All that goes through my head now is that Gordon Lightfoot song, *The Wreck of the Edmund Fitzgerald.*

The next time the buzzer sounds, it is not the stalker. It’s the police asking questions I can barely contemplate through an intercom.

“Does he have a weapon?” they ask me.

“I didn’t see one.”

“Have you seen him before?”

“No.”

“From what you told 9-1-1, he answers the description of a man who’s been raping women around here at knifepoint about once a month. He must live in a nearby building because we are never fast enough to catch him.”

“Is there any place in this world that is safe for a woman alone at night?” I ask him.

"Never has been, never will be probably. But don't think guys around here don't have problems. It happens to them, too."

I'd never thought about that.

"That's it, then," the cop says to me as I study him through the peephole.

"I guess so," I answer. "You don't need more specifics, more follow-up?"

"You might want to post flyers on the street to alert your neighbors," he suggests. "It would be a good service to let them know what happened. This kind of thing happens all the time, but in this case, you were lucky."

"Thank you," I tell him, thinking back to how my legs ran just at the right moment without any conscious input from my conflicted brain. "And thank you, dear legs, too."

"What?" the policeman asks.

"Nothing," I say, "Just talking to myself. Thanks again. I'll do the flyers. I promise."

And I did.

THE "ALMOST" ABDUCTION OF BABY SUSIE

At 43 years old, I find myself in the maternity ward of an Anchorage, Alaska hospital – forgetting why I am here. At a routine check-up a few days before, my obstetrician had asked me: "Would you like to have your baby on Tuesday or Thursday?

Looking forward to the birth of Susie for all these months (but apparently deeply in the midst of a condition called pre-eclampsia), my life and the baby's life are in jeopardy; the time is now.

"That's a little like asking if I want to get my leg cut off today or tomorrow," I joke, knowing that the difference is that at the end I'll have a healthy baby. But I am so afraid of the pain of childbirth that I have even hired a doula to go through the process with me. And now, on Tuesday, it will all begin.

"I almost lost my faith in God," the doula says a few days later. "If God had taken you, that would have killed my faith."

She says this because she knows the risks I am willing to take to have Susie. Tuesday arrives and I am splayed out on a birthing table trying to get things rolling, but I jump around so much that I squish the epidural needle in my spine. This completely stops the flow of the anesthetic. Feeling empathetic, the young anesthesiologist jumps in, pumping so much pain-saving liquid into my veins that within seconds, I flatline. The last thing I remember is my ex-husband talking sports over my quivering belly while the ready-for-anything male nurse looks on.

When my eyes roll back in my head, the professionalism of the staff kicks in but so does the weirdness. When it's all over, I am moved to a recovery room but I can't quite grasp what is happening. I am on so many drugs for so long, I forget that I've even had a baby. One of the nurses admonishes me for this, saying:

"Your baby's been crying for hours. Don't you want to see her?"

Well, of course I want to see her! Are you kidding me?

Pulling myself together, I call from my bed to the doorway where little Susie is crying softly in the arms of the nurse.

THE "ALMOST" ABDUCTION OF BABY SUSIE

"Come over here, sweetheart," I say. "It's okay, you can stop crying. Mommy's here."

The sound of my voice reaches those little ears and Susie recognizes me! I can see her trying to wiggle in my direction as the nurse places her in the crook of my arm. Once there, she settles down, staring up at me, already responsive and bright. So far, we've both survived to tell the tale. But in the morning, the nurse they assign to me makes me wonder.

"Your daughter looks just like me," she says as she wheels me into a different private room on new doctor's orders.

"You mean *me*, right?"

She doesn't respond except to say that she has orders to move me to a darkened room, no visitors or phone calls, food intake limited to water and popsicles, and observation by full-time, round-the-clock RNs like her.

"Am I in bad shape?" I ask her. "Why is this happening?"

"It's just for observation," she says. "It won't last more than 48 hours, probably less."

I don't even remember seeing my husband since the birth.

Hours pass and, along with it, countless scary more conversations with the RN who barely allows me to hold Susie because she might "upset" me.

To pass the time, I watch TV and play soothing music like the flute music of Paul Horn on my Walkman. But when I see a segment on Oprah on the stealing of babies from hospitals by medical personnel, I get downright scared. *What timing!* As Oprah ticks off the tell-tale warning signs of a potential abduction, some signs fit. Surely, I am just zonkers from medications, hormones and a crazy birth experience. What if I report a professional RN for casing my baby when I might be simply out of my mind? The timing to have me watched must have ended because a couple of nurses arrive to pull open the heavy drapes, disconnect the catheter and needle in my arm, bring Susie and her things to my bedside on rollers, and slap a steak dinner with chocolate cheesecake on my food tray. *What?* After only a liquid diet for the last two days, even the sight of a Diet Cherry Coke makes me upchuck.

But the good news is Susie and I are going home and the scary nurse is not on duty as we leave. I never do get much of an explanation for all that isolation except some vague comments about kidney disfunction.

Once home, it isn't long before the scary nurse calls, saying she misses Susie and wants to come over to our house. I never gave her my home number or address and the hospital did not say anything about home care. I am getting more and more concerned about her actions and what they might mean. The time has come to figure out if I should call her supervisor. But if I do, I could be making a huge mistake.

"Maybe we can have lunch in a couple of weeks," I say during one call from the nurse in question. "Let's meet at a restaurant because by then I'll be desperate to get out of the house."

"Oh, no," she says. "I'm off today, how about noon? I have all these special presents for your baby. You must have noticed that Susie is an old soul. She is amazing! She could be my baby, you know."

"No," I say, "she's not your baby. Have you tried adoption?"

"My husband won't agree to it," she answers. "I tried. A lot."

I hang up and dial the hospital. "It could just be my hormones," I say. "I'm pretty wonky from childbirth and the flatlining and all. But I swear I never gave her my home phone number or address; did you? I don't want to cast any shadows on a career caregiver but I did see this thing on Oprah when I was in the hospital about infant abductions by medical personnel and I'm scared."

"I need to know everything you remember that she did and said to you," the supervisor says. "At the very least, we have a nurse in crisis."

"Makes sense to me," I tell her.

THE "ALMOST" ABDUCTION OF BABY SUSIE

This is a very wise supervisor. We agree that she will keep an eye on the woman without mentioning us, but also definitely reassign her away from maternity.

"Leave it to me," she says assuredly.

I never hear anything more about this situation or the nurse. And I am too wrapped up in motherhood to have a need to pursue it.

A few months later, I discover I am pregnant again and our little family is off and running.

But I do think of the nurse sometimes, wondering if I did the right thing and if she ever found what she was looking for – in a good way, of course.

Art & Music

Ted Bob's beautiful guitar playing

Karlyn Eckman's beautiful artwork
(as appreciated by Jim Bob Craig)

International Music Blogger
Mitzi Beliveau and guitarist Jim Stairs

He hits
the high notes
like a devil and
the low notes
like a god.

Spoony

SPOONY
SURF
COMPANY
Sister
RESTROOM
PARTY ON!

Ralph McTell

RALPH MCTELL

One evening, when I was a young music student, guitar forever at my side, I find myself in London in the rafters at the Bloomsbury Theater at a Ralph McTell concert *(Concert #1).* His rich, masculine sound and presence have eked their way into my swiss-cheese heart. Already famous for the song *Streets of London*, every card-carrying folkie with any self-respect sings it every chance they get. And although I wildly and consummately love all of Ralph's music (and tally many hours of free time lost in it), there is one song I think of as "ours," one song that I loop incessantly – an obscure album track called *Grand Affaire.*

(With music, you can dream anything you want.)

Would Ralph somehow telepathically sense my presence at his concert and magically pull *Grand Affaire* from his repertoire and sing it to me alone tonight? *Right.* This fantasy is right up there with kissing Paul McCartney (a dream that millions of other baby boomers like me probably still have!) Frustrated, I start a conversation with the older woman in the seat next to me. She has a great idea:

"Why don't you write a note and put it by his microphone? Maybe he'll see it, honey."

The woman is even digging in her purse for pen and paper for me!

So, I write the note, run down to the stage between sets, and because it's in the realm of fantasy, completely forget about it.

But Ralph doesn't.

After he sings a few other moving songs, he stops, looks out at the audience, and says: "This one is for Diane."

Heaven!

But that is not the end of this story.

Fast forward 35 years and I am preparing to visit London again with my new husband – and we discover that Ralph McTell is on tour in Great Britain. Of all the tantalizing towns where we can see him play, we wisely choose Cardigan, Wales because I've heard that it is fun and historic to visit, especially the café across from the castle. As luck would have it, we had scored three choice tickets for Ralph's concert venue across town *(Concert #2)* and we end up front row center. To me, this is a sign, but to my husband (the lead guitarist in a country/rock band who has never heard of Ralph McTell), the whole thing is "meh."

A few days before this, Paul, another musician friend (who fronts the band my husband plays in), joins us in London from rural Minnesota. The three of us (with me the only excited one) drive all the way to Wales, taking our seats at Ralph's feet at the Mwldan Theater in Cardigan, a name that none of us can pronounce.

This time, I've written the note about *Grand Affaire* in advance including an arrow pointing to my seat right in front of center stage. But Ralph is more famous now and the stage is bigger; I can't reach his microphone to leave a note. A roadie moving instruments on the stage before the concert accepts the message from me. Smiling a smile that looks suspiciously like Ralph's (of course at this point in my obsession I would have thought Colonel Sanders looked like Ralph), I wonder: Could this young man be his grown son Tom? I swear, in Ralph's first minute onstage, he looks briefly down in my direction but alas, he goes through the entire evening without singing my song.

Sadness!

As he's about to close the show, he pauses and says: "Wait! There is one more song I want to remember to sing before *Streets of London*." He then says those five touching words that meant so much to me 35 years ago in London and now do so, again in Wales:

"This one is for Diane."

But the story doesn't end there either!

I am not a stalker. I am not even a person who lives on another planet most of the time. But the following year, my husband and I discover that Ralph is headlining a week-long Costa Festival at a hotel in Portugal *(Concert #3)*. It will be nearly round-the-clock music, all you can eat meals and all the jamming on the guitar my husband could want. So, it isn't long before Jim and I are sitting at an elegant white dinner table in the Algarve with Jayne and Ron, two strangers from the north of England. (However uppity this sounds, you have to remember that we are not rich people. We saved up!)

Jayne & Ralph

"Why did you choose this particular festival?" I ask Jayne, trying to make conversation. "It's amazing how many festivals you get to choose from in the U.K. every year."

She does not hesitate.

"Ralph."

"Ralph? You mean Ralph McTell? Us, too! You'd love the story about how he sang a song for me 35 years ago in London and then again in Wales last year."

"He did that for me, too," Jayne says. "Twice!" Jayne pulls out her phone and shows me photos from two different times in her youth – with a younger Ralph's arms wrapped around her shoulders both times. I only have one picture like that. And it's less than a year old. Hoping I'm not being masochistic, I take a chance: "Do you have a favorite song he sings for you, Jayne?"

"You first," she says kindly. This isn't a competition (it's more of a love fest), but we both already know it's going to be the same song. We might as well say it out loud: "It's *Grand Affaire*, right?"

"Are you kidding me?" I say. "We are twin sisters of different mothers! Who else knows that song but us?"

That of course is a very short-sighted perspective, but the story doesn't end there, either!

Not one hour later, walking through the lobby of the hotel, there he is, Ralph McTell himself, flanked by his hardworking son, Tom. I try to look the other way so as not to bother them, but to my horror, Tom beckons us over. He does this because earlier I had run into him in an elevator (although *cornering* might be more accurate) and he confirmed to me that he is Ralph's son. Also in the elevator (it was a long ride), I gave him a "little something" I'd made to pass on to his dad. Being called over now means that I'm going to have to talk to Ralph McTell directly for the first time and I'm 71-years-old!

Switching to an internal monologue, I ask myself the obvious question: "What does your age have to do with anything?" (It's that mind-body split that happens to me sometimes when I'm in a crisis.) This time, the crisis is that I am made stupid by raw talent in any field of art, any field really. I need a quick strategy to get through this chance meeting or I might end up speaking in uncontrollable babble or laugh hysterically into my hand in front of Ralph and Tom.

"Just think of him naked!" I advise myself, fully aware that Ralph is probably as much a flawed human being as any of us.

"Naked? Who? Tom? Or Ralph?"

"Wrong direction, girl!" I self-correct. "How about picturing both of them in Santa suits?"

RALPH MCTELL

"Yes, that works" – but just then Tom interrupts my inner antics with a formal introduction. (This is Europe after all.)

"This is Diane, Dad. "She has a gift for you."

Ralph answers: "Oh, really now?"

This inspires Tom to action, and he pulls out the little black pouch I left in his care in the elevator and motions for me to hand it directly to his father. Ralph undoes the tie at the top of the pouch and pulls out the pin button inside. But as he places what Brits call the pin "badge" in his hand, his look is curious, quizzical, unsure.

"The *smell* of the sheets and the feel of the wine?" he reads thoughtfully.

"Yes," I say proudly. "I made the button myself."

But my inner editor senses from Ralph's expression that something is not right here.

"Please don't tell me I got the lyrics wrong?"

"Well, only partially, dear. It's the *taste* of the sheets and the feel of the wine, I'm afraid. Not so much the *smell."*

"*The smell*? Oh, my God," I say to him and everyone else nearby. "Could I have gotten that any more wrong?"

"You were close. You *almost* got it right. No worries."

"Can I make you a new button and send it to you in England?" I ask.

"That would be lovely!" he responds. (From his body language, he is clearly ready to move on.)

RALPH MCTELL

"Just one more thing, Ralph? It's very important. I bet you didn't know that 36 years ago at the Bloomsbury Theater in London, you sang *Grand Affaire* just for me. And then again last year in Cardigan, Wales, you did the same thing. I can't tell you how much that means to me."

"Well, then, I'll just have to sing it for you again on Saturday night! What is your husband's name? Jim? I hope I can remember that until Saturday."

"It's okay," I say back to him. "Diane is good enough."

A short time later, on a bar deck overlooking the Atlantic Ocean, I lament to Jim not only about how I got Ralph's lyrics wrong on the button, but also how I'd thrown my own husband under the bus in the name department. I was so nervous, I didn't even get a chance to ask Ralph if he could sing *Grand Affaire* to Jayne, too. Just then, I feel a disturbance in the force. Somehow I fear that things are about to get worse.

Oh, no. Oh sh--, really sh--?" I say.

Someone is standing over me and reaching for my hand from a position above my patio chair. Of course, it is the Man Himself who just happens to be heading to the bar for a beer and overhears me.

"Don't fret, my dear! It was a lovely gesture for you to make that button for me. Enjoy yourself!"

Now that one hand is resting in Ralph McTell's hand and the other is in my husband Jim's, I'm good for a long, long time – maybe a lifetime?

The Saturday night concert on the Main Stage rolls around and, true to his word, Ralph tells the crowd (just before singing *Grand Affaire),* that "This song is for my lovely American friends, Diane and Jim." And since we are the only Yanks in a group of about 800 Brits, whenever anyone hears our accents that evening, we are not only Ralph's friends, we are everybody's friends!

GRAND AFFAIRE *by Ralph McTell*

Remember the moon on the wall, didn't she shine?
The taste of the sheets and the feel of the wine
Wasn't I glad that you was mine
In the Grand Affaire?

Ralph McTell
To Diane
35 years on!
Love

LOCAL MUSICIANS, LOCAL HEROES

I once read that a musician is someone who puts $5,000 worth of gear into a $500 car to drive 100 miles to a $50 gig.

All over the world, in the largest cities and tiniest villages, awesome, talented musicians and bands make music for us out of love – and because they can. If lucky, they receive at least some money and recognition for their efforts.

But some artists feel diminished because they give so much yet never become rich or famous. I say your contributions to our lives are greater than that. You make us feel joy that we don't always feel, remember people and places we have long forgotten (or are just discovering). You connect us to our humanity every day. You make us feel happy!

Do you realize how important this is?

Rick

Tom

THE RELUCTANT PIONEER

Tom and Carol live the good life, as life goes, creative and musical. The force behind a blues band called *The Cobras*, Tom plays the harmonica from his heart to his toes and back again. If you are lucky enough to hear his band you just have to get up and dance.

As a couple, Tom & Carol have faith and love, great senses of humor and the cleanest, most organized house in the Twin Cities. *And they volunteer!*

Even so, not long ago Tom got sick. Most of his friends, although similar in age, had not quite hit that stage of life yet; we all scrambled to help. Somehow fate picked Tom first and, rather than fading away with his diagnosis (with Carol's hard work and devotion), Tom rallied. He's learned to walk again; he's trained his brain to think better; and best of all, he continues to sing and play the blues to all of his appreciative audiences in the Twin Cities. A bit embarrassed by the metal music stand he sometimes uses to display the lyrics, he seems to consider its presence a weakness. But to those of us who have watched his brave recovery, we know it is a strength. Both Tom and Carol are heroes to their friends because they love and support each other and the community. They never give up. Something will get all of us eventually, as we all know, but Tom has been an exemplary pioneer in this crazy world. And man, not to be underestimated, he sure can play a mean and soulful mouth harp!

Two famous
opera singers
(Linda, Sylvia & Me)

SYLVIA B. DAVIS – A MEMORIAL (1935-2022)

With Friend Jan

"Luck is what happens when preparation meets opportunity. I loved singing. It was a pleasure and an honor to create two roles written for me by major composers Gian Carlo Menotti and Andrew Imbrie. Having a career gave me the opportunity to be in the company of superlative singers, conductors, musicians, directors, coaches, all of it. To work at that level where people are really fine musicians and talents is very lucky and satisfying. It is more than satisfying." – Sylvia B. Davis

Sylvia B. Davis was a decorated opera singer and voice teacher who lived and loved fiercely. A true diva, she was once fired by a major West Coast opera company for having an affair with the conductor, the love of her life. When they reconnected 50 years later, they married instantly, spent 8 years together until he died at his beach house on Long Island to the sound of crashing waves. Sylvia's exit at age 83 was just as dramatic – cancer, three doctors' appointments, and a cup of poison later and she was gone. With her was her little kitty Mischa, a nurse, and her beloved sons. And in the shadows, if you will, were her life's audience of friends and lovers. RIP, Sylvia. You are loved.

WOMAN WITH SHOULDERS *(Song)*

Woman with shoulders
Crying tears on a heavy breast
Seeking warmth and comfort in kind
Unwinding her braided hair
Behind a shadow somewhere
Creeping softness draws
A lover's hand to mind.

A child born, at times a mother's scorn
Upon a painted palette merge
the colors of her day.
She never asks to answer
She who only knows the creeping softness
When it draws a lover's hand away.

You can go and ask the lady
Though she never speaks to answer
For her arms and hands are shaking
Through the colors she is painting

And the tears she has collected
In a bucket by the creaking door
Of the tower where she watches
And the cats that climb the ladders
And the red-checkered curtains
She goes dancing in a softness
As her candles go on burning at both ends.

Ferron

FOLK MUSIC IS DEAD

In 1979, I move to NYC to make it as a singer-songwriter. To help my education along, I register at NYU's music department but quickly find that much of the appetite for my kind of music is gone. Although there are still remnants of the famous Greenwich Village coffee club scene in my NYU neighborhood, and people like Mary Grace still hire folk singers at church venues uptown, life has moved on to punk, disco and who knows what else.

That's fair, change is awesome. But are those of us, whose only sin is being out of step with time, destined to sing only in the shower? Like in folk music, spectacle is not my thing:

Heart is.
Expression is.
Connecting is.

So, I bury myself in the demands of the Gallatin Division of NYU. And although there does seem to be little hope for me to find an audience in the new world order, I sing to please myself and a small circle of friends.

Walking the village one night (there is nothing like the streets of New York City with time on your hands), I see a simple but interesting sign on the Gerdes Folk City marquee:

"Ferron"

I'm intrigued but I have no idea what to expect. With $7 in my pocket (and a $7 cover), I empty my wallet and secure a small cocktail table up front. Digging up loose change for a Diet Coke, I settle in with a very low bar of satisfaction that soon turns into blood-red rage when Ferron takes the stage.

Overtakes is a better word.

All leather and attitude, she commands respect. That's fine; I've seen that before. But being a fellow folk singer only days apart in age (according to a flyer on the wall), I spend more time than I should apologizing to the world for being 10 years too late in sound and style. But not Ferron! Unapologetic as hell, she opens her mouth and out comes – not *Jimmy-Crack-Corn* (although that has its place), but songs, original folk songs – like the one about the factory job where some people had worked there longer than she'd been alive. Or other particularly moving songs about losing her shoes or how she wondered if, as the conductor on her train went about his daily business, he hid his fiddle in the back?

I have an imagination, too. And watching Ferron command the stage – and hearts – of a contemporary New York audience makes me angry as hell. Not at her, of course (I am ga-ga over her music), but at me for accepting the status quo and for not trying harder to be heard. Ferron's music is *real* folk music, GREAT folk music, but seeing her this way is a particularly painful awakening for me and my imagination throws a fit. Picking up the little cocktail table in front of me, Diet Coke and all, I throw it against a back wall and walk out, tipping my hat to Ferron as I go, picking dead flowers in Washington Square Park and not even trying to revive them when I get home. Or maybe none of this happened at all? Folk music may be dead in Greenwich Village – then and now – but Ferron, for one, proves that it is still alive in a million living rooms and a million hearts everywhere, no matter what it is called.

Jim Bob & Stacey

Pam

KATE WOLF

KATE WOLF

It is Christmas season 1986 and I am in New York City trying to make it as a singer-songwriter when I hear about it. With my guitar slapping perennially against my right knee, I slip into a yellow cab on the way to a gig. I repeat this motion so often, it is already the start of a future varicose vein on my leg.

"What kind of music do you play?" the driver in the turban asks.

"Irish; mostly my own stuff and some Kate Wolf," I answer.

"Ah, Kate Wolf. California. You know about her, do you?"

"Oh, yes," I say. "You, too? I used to go to her shows at the West of the Laguna in Sebastopol. I am so in love with how she 'breathes in' Sonoma County and exhales it into beautiful song. I was studying music at the local college then, and wasn't very far along on the guitar yet. Sometimes I would call her to make sure I had the chords right. I particularly loved *The Red Tail Hawk* and rang her up once to double-check the chords. With only a slight hint of judgment, she told me: 'The chords to that song are Em and G, Diane.'"

(I love that she knows my name.)

"That's all the chords in the song, Kate?" I ask her.

"That's all."

I take a beat. "Maybe I could have figured that out by myself?" I laughed to her.

Kate stayed kind.

"So, do you know what happened to her?" the driver asks again.

"Know what?" I answer. We hadn't quite reached the Irish pub where I am playing but I know that something sad is coming and I'm not sure I want to hear it.

"Kate died today. Leukemia. It was in the news."

"She's only 44!" I say woefully as if the driver can change the truth.

"So, that's that," I think to myself, climbing out of the taxi and tipping the driver well. In honor of Kate, I march into the pub like many of us all over the world still do today, and sing her songs like there is no tomorrow.

Lynyrd Skynyrd

FREE BIRD

At a job organizing fun outings for customers at the Mall of America, rarely does the fickle Minnesota weather impact *anything* that I've planned. Minnesotans are hearty, to be sure, but on this day, we have to pay attention.

A tornado warning has cleared the Radisson Blu building and all of us with it. Since it is my first evacuation, I am just as scared as everyone else. Corralling the masses, we all stand under the hotel overhang, peering at green patches of sky through gaps in the concrete parking garage nearby.

All around me, people cluster together talking and laughing with a few in tears from fear. What I don't exactly notice is the actual group of men surrounding me until I switch from "Customer Protective Mode" into "Be Here Now." These guys are definitely not Minnesotans, I chuckle to myself, surveying their more than "artistic" personas. Dressed in jeans and leather – all of a certain age – they hold oddly shaped objects that I soon recognize as guitar cases and other musical things. I play guitar, too, and am about to talk capos and minor chords when I catch sight of one man's briefcase. Slung over his shoulder, its leather strap is tooled with an oddly spelled name that at first, doesn't register:

"Lynyrd Skynyrd"

If these guys are concert-goers, I'm not at all surprised that they have the bucks to hole up at the Rad Blu. Some people find that it's cheaper to fly to concerts in Europe than to pay American prices. With all of the band paraphernalia these guys are holding, they must either be super fans – or the band itself.

I come to my senses: These guys are the real thing, flushed out of the safety of their hotel rooms by an errant tornado. Eyeing each man separately (especially the one with waist-length gray hair), I realize that I am standing in a sea of Lynyrd Skynyrd members! As I ponder this, my eyes lock in recognition with the one who was so striking that he could not be ignored: Rickey Medlocke himself. (I know this because I looked up the band later.) The look in his eyes is not the expected "Hello, love" or "Back at ya."

Instead, he looks terrified! Of what? Me?

I have never been a rock star but I can see that, especially in a tornado scare like this, I wouldn't like women screaming and hyperventilating over me under a swaying hotel overhang. In truth, I have only heard one of their songs, *Free Bird,* but I can't sing it and I'm not even sure who wrote it. So Rickey Medlocke (if it *is* Rickey Medlocke) and Gary Rossington (the guy with the briefcase) – actually all of them – are totally safe with me. Maybe.

"No problem," I say to Rickey, keeping my distance but also gearing up to say completely the wrong thing as usual. "If you were Paul McCartney, I'd be all over you."

As full force winds rage nearby, Rickey has no idea what I am capable of around famous people. Or maybe he sensed it? My old boyfriend (who helped Jack Nicholson with authenticity on the film "The Last Detail") knew. He refused to take me up to Jack's house in the Hollywood Hills because I turn completely stupid over inspired artistic talent. Starting with screaming my lungs out at the Beatles on TV in my youth, I have even recently planned to take a portable chair to Paul McCartney's office in London to wait (for however long it takes) for him to magically appear and finally ask me to marry him. This is half a century after the Beatles landed at JFK and eight years after I married my perfect husband, Jim.

Like Juliet, my love is enduring and true and I am not alone!

"Thanks for understanding," is all Rickey says back to me as the tornado scare passes and we are all cleared to go back into the building. "Not up for any of that fan shit right now."

"I know what you mean," I say, lacing my arm around his back.

"Can I have your autograph anyway?"

The Bad Ass Boots
Pat & Billie D, Joyce Baker, Billie B & Shazam

Billie & Lisa Victorious in Concert! (Bad Ass Boots)

MUSIC SAVES: ARE WE ON TO SOMETHING?

When it comes to extracurricular activities most of us age out of bars and clubs while others attend church on Zoom, religiously watch *Wheel of Fortune* and *Jeopard*y (okay, we do, too), and take all afternoon to check the mail. I remember watching a couple slightly older than me, Bruce and Mary Jo, jump gleefully from one music venue to the other in retirement, often posting favorite song videos online. How do these magnificent appreciators stay awake so late, so often? Why do they look so happy?

Jim Bob, my 76-year old husband, plays lead guitar in a country/rock band that does more than 100 gigs a year. Up some nights until 3 AM, we both struggle through the 4th set but he never complains and I never get tired of his music. He's following his muse, his passion. Playing music invigorates and inspires him. He's grown his hair, changed his look and buys more guitars and gadgets than ever. He loves to talk shop with other musicians. He enjoys helping to bring musical joy to southern Minnesota. He's happiest when he's playing and I'm happy to be part of it.

The same is true of our friend Franny, another consummate appreciator, who joins me one night for pizza at the Main Street Bistro in Guerneville, California. Tonight, the owner Suzi has booked *The Bad Ass Boots,* an awe-inspiring group of musicians from the Bay Area who pull us in as fans from the first song. Between sets, we want to get to know them as people, and now, five years later, we are still friends. As I said, some of us feel that in our "laters," social connections wane.

MUSIC SAVES: ARE WE ON TO SOMETHING?

But for us, the timeless wonder of music protects us against all of that. These may not actually be "The Golden Years," as advertised, but this much is true: We are freer now than we have ever been, regardless of health and family issues. It just takes some of us a lifetime to figure out how to jimmy the lock on the cage with music as the inspiration!

Billie D and Shazam of The Bad Ass Boots

The Paul Stewart Show

Passing the Torch to Young Caleb with Grandma Jean

Stephanie &
Nate
Liz
Kristie & Paul
METALLICA
Ed & Jean
Stumpy & Kris
MASTER MUSIC
APPRECIATORS!
Bruce
Kit
Molly
Mary Jo
Vickie
Jason
These fans show up!

BURIED TREASURE *(Song)*

The crystal bowl is filled with ice
And fresh cut lemon wedges
The pattern is diamond-shaped
And rough around the edges
I put it on a table with three roses
and a spoon
As the family portraits hang around
The crowded room

CHORUS
Rough around the edges
So cool and crystal clear
Like diamonds in the rough we live
Year to year
We are like buried treasure
On the eve of its return
The value not yet realized
The payoff yet unearned

Nana, she grew roses
in the tenement years
Papa knew his business
But was motivated by fear
Still he made a living
Under the shadow of demise
Wondering if he'd lose it all
Before he won the prize

I slip into a cotton dress
Soft against my skin
And sit down on the hardwood floor
To look around again
I pull a pillow off a chair
And lay down for awhile
And close my weary eyes
Under my grandmother's smile.

Bob K of The Legendary Titilators

Al & Joanne

RIP Prince: Award-winning seed art by Susie

Thoughtful &
Inspiring

LOOK AGAIN

"The successful revolutionary is a statesman, the unsuccessful one a criminal." – *Erich Fromm*

The father of my children is a Quaker man from a highly educated Minneapolis family who loves the arts. Regularly, we attended various art car parades, musical events and plays as a group. Sometimes we even put on our own productions. Mostly this was exciting and fun. But sometimes it created painful learning opportunities for me.

Having moved to New York City in my youth to make it as a singer-songwriter, I sing my heart out in the bars and coffee houses of Greenwich Village. I study hard at NYU for my Master's degree (just in case). By doing this, I assimilate standards that are almost impossible for most humans to achieve.

Excellence is the thing in New York City. We expect and revere it. Everyone strives for it and some actually succeed. But if something isn't good, it isn't worth doing, right? Picture that wonderful Simon and Garfunkel free concert in Central Park – or a Taylor Swift concert – but out of synch. If it's bad enough, free or not, New York audiences will pan it, make a big deal out of it to the negative, boo the performance and leave. It doesn't matter who it is.

One time, when our extended family gathers at a local Minneapolis community playhouse, the play is awful. Having seen productions on/off Broadway, the West End and more, I cringe when adults can't act, forget lines, props on stage don't work, doors don't open, singers go flat and the trumpet player can't find his groove.

But when I look at the family members around me, they are smiling – not appalled at all! *They are enthralled!* Clapping and singing along, they seem 100% engaged, enjoying every moment. For me, it's like trying to meditate in a quiet room with a construction crew working outside. Didn't anyone get the memo?

For my family, it turns out that something doesn't have to be perfect to exist, it can just exist. If you want to sing or dance, and

LOOK AGAIN

you are awful at it, do it anyway! No judgment here! But how can this be? If we lower our expectations, won't we be destined to endure the mundane? While they have a great time at the play, I'm miserable, counting the minutes until I can gracefully bow out.

I have standards! Don't they?

Are they so unsophisticated artistically that they can't plainly see the inadequacies in front of them? Or, could it be that I have never learned to tolerate – or celebrate – human imperfection? Do I have a need to prove to everyone that I am smart enough to know good art from bad art?

Am I a snob?

Whether we are talking art, body image, writing or restaurant personnel, there is another possible approach: "Be here now." Somewhat akin to Stephen Stills' concept of "Love the One You're With," there can be joy in error. If an experience is not top notch, "Get over yourself," I now tell myself. "Look again!"

Within most people, you can always find some good. It's the same with art, and more broadly, life. And if you are actually capable of magnificence, do that, too. Everyone is invited to the party! If you are feeling miserable at an event and need a self-test to ensure that you don't make the same mistakes I've made, ask yourself this question: What am I missing here?

Mina, Avram & Greg

Raquel & Frank

JAX'S MEDITATION

Our dog Jax, partly Chihuahua and partly Jack Russell Terrier, loves McDonald's. About once a month he gets to "free bark" all the way through the drive-up window, have one sausage patty in pieces, and then climbs up on my lap to watch the birds and ducks out the window. I have not found any time limit to his patience on this activity. When we finally go home, we take a nice walk, have a good mutual howl (his favorite trick), and a cuddly nap. *Ah, doggies. Don't you love them?*

PIN BUTTON HEAVEN

A proud moment as a world citizen came at a sad time when the father of my supervisor at The College of Saint Scholastica passed away at nearly 96 years of age. Unbeknownst to me, the pin buttons I made for his Minnesota memorial traveled across the world to Cameroon, Africa for his burial there. Papa's loving, highly educated but humble immigrant daughter, Dr. Doreene, is a quiet hero in her own right in her roles as teacher-of-teachers, committed mother and friend.

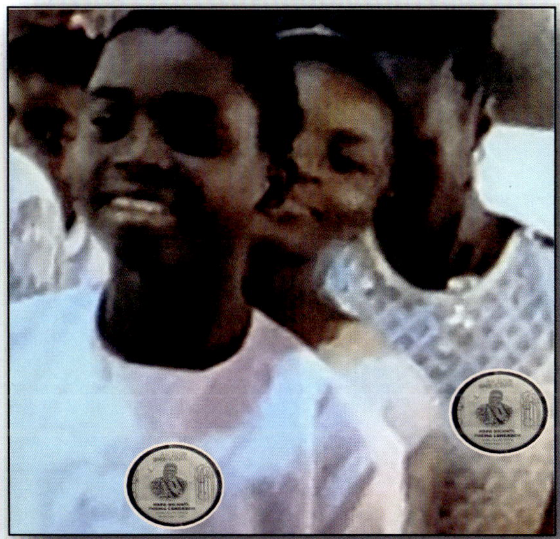

Ruthie, community hero and organizer, exercising with Hazel

STAY TUNED

Seventy-three years on, I have a theory about this world. This theory comes from experience – knowing me, knowing you. It is not the only theory, don't let anyone tell you it is. It does not victimize or blame or try to make us smaller than we are. It does not sacrifice our sanity to fear or our power to forces (or people) outside of ourselves. It is very human; just how things are. This theory is simply:

I know things. So do you.

Life is hard, requiring so much wisdom, skill and thought to get it right that, sometimes, we cave. In our fear of facing how small we really are (and how big), we are the *Emperor's New Clothes*, pretending to be larger than we are, or worse – allowing other people or things to be large for us. Even when we fall in love, sometimes we want our lover to take over the world for us, leaving us to float freely, to be big in the moments when we feel insufficient and small. If this goes on too long, to where we no longer have power, the costs are high but the need stays strong.

Beyond this theory, beyond everything, is the human heart. Heart transcends all fears and limitations. It transcends *everything.* It does not require anything earthly to love. To feel. To dance.

Life is so cynical – I mean cyclical – that sometimes it takes total devastation for the heart cycle to come around again. It's just a matter of time. Hang in there, have faith and stay tuned.

CATHOLICS VS. PRODS

As a kid, after reading every book under the sun about Catholic saints, I conclude that with so many poor people in the world, I do not need Christmas presents. Each year on the morning after Christmas, before anyone can catch me, I take my best present (except for the guitar in fourth grade that is too precious) and leave it behind the statue of the Virgin Mary at church.

It takes years to realize (after studying the behavior of my Protestant friends), that there is an alternative to martyrdom. At age 12, I develop a theory on what I perceive to be the difference between Protestants and Catholics: If a "Prod" is given two oranges, they give one to the poor – and keep the other to sustain themselves! *Really?*

If a Catholic (let's say a Catholic like me) is gifted two oranges, apples, or whatever, we immediately gift *both* to the poor and in some cases, end up dying alone, destitute and hungry, of no real value to anyone except maybe 100 years later as the subject of another book on the lives of the saints.

Seventy-plus years on, I still have the tendency to give things away, much to the chagrin of my two (consecutive) Protestant husbands. In fact, I want to give this book away to you right now! It only goes to prove that you can take the Catholic out of the church, but rarely, even after a lifetime of living, can you take the church out of a Catholic!

By Uncle Damon Cuccia

MY MOTHER'S SKATEBOARD

My nephew Dan always had a secret but most of us never knew what it was. When he was 5, his mom Linda P. got sick, asking her friends Mina and Greg to take Dan home to live with them if the worst happened. Dan was the product of a neighborhood hookup; his dad lived nearby. Years later, with no real contact or interest from this bio dad, Dan endures the news that all hope for a future relationship with him is lost. His bio dad, like his mother, has also passed away too young. And while Mina and Greg step in and love Dan for the rest of his life, he is technically an orphan. His inheritance from Linda P. (the significance of which is never lost on her thoughtful son), is her skateboard. This was her passion. Dan knew that it meant much more to her than the wood and wheels it was made of. And then a good thing happened; Mina became pregnant with Avram and now Dan had a brother. They remain close to the end, Dan's end, because like his bio parents, Dan never sees 40.

Through the years, by design and accident, Dan and I get together over shrimp and conversation. My favorite time with him was when he asked, as a teenager, for me to drive him behind Target to watch him practice his beloved skateboard. Later, as an intelligent and rebellious teenager, he is made famous on the TV Show *Wife Swap* as part of Mina and Greg's "peacenik" family. The other wife, a military spouse, tells Dan that if he doesn't cut his long hair, she will seize his skateboard. His answer reverberates through the air waves. "If you take my skateboard, I will burn your bible." I don't think the lady ever knew that the skateboard was Dan's only physical connection to his mother.

One time, driving to Wisconsin, Dan tells me not to let on to his parents that he actually does love them and listens (although does not always respond) to everything they tell him.

The next part is hard to take in and understand:

One day, not long ago, Dan hikes into a beautiful grove of trees in Minneapolis and kills himself with a gun. Again, the worst has happened.

Dan was a hard worker who was loved, cared for, interacted with and celebrated by his adoptive family. The street fair held in his honor attracted hundreds of neighbors and friends. But for 15 years, Dan had struggled to find that place of peace, that place we all search for of self-acceptance and, I'm guessing, acceptance of the world. Dan rode his skateboard many times into his own nirvana, but this time, he did not come back. When someone told me how Dan had passed, lyrics from a Don McLean song repeated

Art by Uncle Damon Cuccia

itself in my head:

"I could have told you (Dan), the world was never meant for one as beautiful as you."

Dan may finally be at peace but he will be forever missed by those who knew him.

LOVE SONG TO ALL THE LOVERS OF THE WORLD (Song)

This is a love song to all the lovers of the world
Looking for new dimensions, answers to your prayers
Some will say they've seen the light of your personal salvation
And who are we to argue with your illuminations?

But I'm scared by all the prophets and appalled by their wealth
I'm agonized by people who totally deny themselves
Ego stands the sinner in the books we all have read
"We only want to end pain," someone said

Now you are dead and how much suffering passed you by?
The answers seem so simple, I could cry
The human race will suffer on, whether feeling it or not
Suffering at times for reasons as we've all been taught

While inside in the soul of you the hunger pains continue
Inside a screaming voice begs to be listened to
But you and I will blot that out because we know what it will do
Simply and clearly it will say "It's up to you"

I meant this as a love song to all the lovers of the world
But I'm angered by the parasites who preyed on your hard times
Who offered you salvation but delivered nursery rhymes
I love you the seekers who can never look back
And I scorn the deceivers
Who lured you off track when you were down

REMEMBERING JONESTOWN

Some people just get it, you know? And sometimes they even follow through.

Decades ago, when Jim Jones caused the death of so many of his believers in Guyana, many of us around the world were devastated by the loss. At the time, I wrote a love song to all of them, a song so sad, I mostly only sang it to myself.

Decades later, visiting friends in Oakland, California, I was told that the graves of hundreds of the People's Temple victims rested just beyond the back fence of their house. "Maybe I can take the words to the song I wrote and post them on a grave?" I mentioned. "I never thought I'd get this close to even knowing the location of their final resting places."

What I picture now is leaving a small piece of paper with the lyrics near the main gravestone in honor of their sacrifices.

"I have a better idea," my friend Billie B. says. She takes me to a place where they blow up my love letter song, mount it on foam board, and laminate it. And 30+ years later, the love song from me to "The People," is finally delivered. RIP.

Billie & Franny

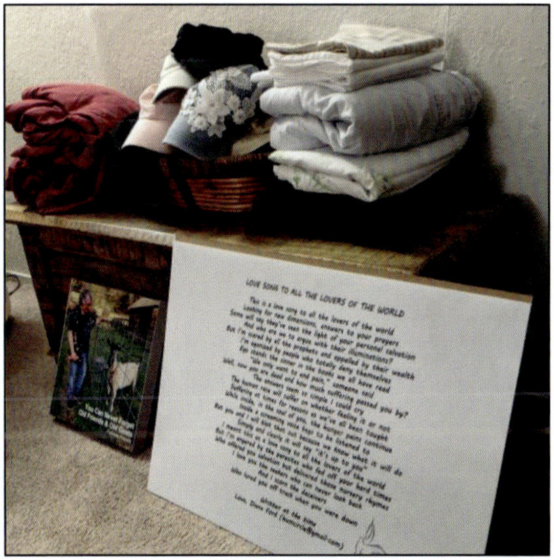

IN MEMORY OF
THE VICTIMS OF
THE JONESTOWN TRAGEDY
NOV. 18, 1978
JONESTOWN, GUYANA
GUYANA EMERGENCY
RELIEF COMMITTEE

DACHAU

Three times I ask people on the street for directions. Three times I get the same response:

"There is no concentration camp here in Dachau."

But I've seen the movies; we all know it is here somewhere. I have an idea: If I can just follow the train tracks – my God, what a painful option retracing your steps is – especially because it works. I pause under the infamous gate with the infamous sign:

"WORK WILL SET YOU FREE"

And sag.

Expecting to cry my heart out for you at first sight, my initial reaction is no reaction at all until I realize that I am being manipulated by color and ambiance. Other than a strip of green grass at the base of a fence, everything is colorless and muted. Even the signature memorial sculpture of human bones near the official museum is easy to miss. Is this an artful downplay designed to keep our emotions in check, to make us feel less outrage when confronted with Germany's first and longest-operating concentration camp? Have they changed this since?

Off to the right, dismantled now to the ground, the only barracks left standing (your barracks), calls to me. I go inside and see the bunk beds (your beds) as they supposedly were when you were imprisoned here.

"Once you see it, little left to know," the docent prompts.

"Yes."

And still no color. I am a South Boston Irish woman turned beach bunny who never met a Jew that I knew of until 1979. But even I can feel it.

Searching for the color of you, I feel pulled magnetically back to the strip of green grass along the fence. Did they allow this to grow when you were here? Did it signify life and hope as it does to me now – or everything they took away from you and what you could no longer have? Or both?

Resting on your blades of grass, probably nourished at one time by the blood of your veins, gently, I sit. Talking to myself out loud, wanting to include you, I wait, in a way you could not wait, and finally rise and stumble into another structure, this one in ruins. It seems that someone *does* understand. Someone does recognize your journey after all. Someone doesn't mind if we feel: A tall red candle, a red, cylindrical vision of spirit, burns brightly for you near the same spot where many of your souls were extinguished; the gas chambers. Silenced until now, three colors remind me your humanity:

*The red of the candle;
*The green of the grass outside;
*The yellow flame of hope that carries us all to heaven.

In my heart, these are colors of remembrance for all oppressed people in the world – then and now. We must never forget.

FAITH & PENNIES

Two days before my flight from Sydney, Australia to the States, I lie down on my bed at a YWCA in Adelaide unsure if I have enough money to pay for the night. Depressed and a little hopeless, I sleep restlessly without a plan, sure that in the morning I will be able to think more clearly.

It has been a year since I left New York for London on a spectacular around-the-world backpacking adventure. Working three times for room and board (twice as a nanny and once cooking on an outback cattle station), money is scarce now and my last stop is the notoriously expensive Honolulu, Hawaii. Without a penny in my pocket, what are my options?

Before I left the States, I had pre-planned two backups: One was to eventually mail a box of office clothes to Hawaii that would help me land a temp job as a legal secretary when I got there. The second one I'd forgotten about completely.

I sleep hard that night in my little narrow bed in Adelaide, knowing I might not be so comfortable tomorrow on empty pockets. When I wake up and my eyes focus, I find that I am staring straight at my travel guitar leaning against the wall like an old friend. *That* was plan number 2! I'd bought it in New York City for $800 in case I got into this exact situation. With it, my logic went, I could either use it to sing for my supper, if necessary, or sell it, if it comes to that. I am saved!

But where does a person sell a guitar super fast in a city that you barely know? Getting the money right away is a prerequisite, I know, as I pack up my stuff and head out on to the street. Without money, I won't get very far.

Working to get my bearings, I cross the street and turn to face the front of the YWCA. Surveying the nearby businesses, I see a tiny cafe to the left – and to the right, unbelievably, a music store! Not thinking I would ever be lucky enough to walk in off the street, sell my guitar, and walk out with enough money to get me home, I hesitate. With nothing to lose, I go in anyway and walk out with $150 Australian dollars! Minutes later, I am sitting in that little café to the left of the YWCA, ordering an egg breakfast and perusing the bus schedule to

Sydney that the waitress pulls from her purse for me. Although I sold the guitar for a fraction of what it was worth, I now have enough money to pay lodging, meals and transportation to the Sydney Airport with $26 and a little change left over. A deep sense of relaxation comes over me – but just a little too soon.

Hours later, I do make it to the Sydney Airport – but with one problem. Yes, I have an around-the-world airline ticket that covers my travel to Honolulu – but apparently there is also a departure tax of $26 I need to pay to leave the country.

"Exactly $26?" I ask the agent at the airport. "Not $24 or $37?"

"$26 it is," she says and I pay the bill. With both contingent plans already in play, I am going to have to eat hardy on the plane and get really creative for a place to stay that night in Honolulu – and even to get around.

Brainstorming plans on the flight, my first thought is the YWCA. I've had really good luck with them when I am low on money. But how do I find a "Y" located somewhere between the Honolulu Airport and downtown? Is there even a downtown Honolulu? Forget buses, those drivers have heard it all. How about a step up from that, a taxi? Maybe look for someone getting into a cab alone, tell them the truth of my situation, and see if I can ride along?

It works! Not only does the businessman I approach share his taxi, he says he knows exactly where the "Y" is located and in minutes, we are on our way there.

Thanking him profusely, I walk into the "Y" and realize pretty quickly that it's a Y<u>M</u>CA not a Y<u>W</u>CA. This means that women are not allowed. Bad news is, I am in the wrong place! Good news is that its only 8 o'clock in the morning. The manager says that if I hurry, there is a temp agency that hires people on a daily basis nearby. This means I can work the day and be paid by the end of it. Perfect! But it is not meant to be. It is no longer a "day" agency. Still, I am planning to temp in Honolulu anyway. It won't hurt to wait in line to talk to someone about getting a job for another day. That someone is a lady, a nice lady, who listens to my story and has an idea: "We aren't a daily temp agency anymore, but I am the night manager of the YWCA on Punahoe and Wilder. If you can get yourself there, I'll make a call to the day manager and we'll see what we can do for you temporarily. Oh – and if she agrees, not only will they house you for the night, the room includes two meals a day and a built-in swimming pool. Here's a little bus money."

Are you kidding me? A pool even?

A few hours later, after convincing the manager that I will be working within five days, I am warm and cozy in a nice twin room over the pool. Just because I can, I check my mailbox because it feels good to have a key to something with my name on it after a full year abroad. Inside, there is a gift envelope from the manager: "Take this to get you through the first week," she writes. "Enclosed is $20 cash. You can pay me back with your first paycheck."

The next day, I check with the temp agency and they have already lined up a job for me at a notoriously quiet Japanese law firm. Once on the clock, secretaries there are not allowed to talk with each other. Chatty by nature, I know this might be the biggest challenge of my whole adventure! Maybe of my life! But why not give it a try?

Retrieving the box of clothes a friend had sent on my behalf to General Delivery, I now have food, shelter, work clothes, bus fare and a job.

And to be fair, I also have skills and an education.

What I learned from this experience, and from my entire year abroad, can be stated in one word:

Faith

Somehow, through many obstacles, I stayed calm, used a little creativity, and believed in myself and other people. With faith and gratitude (plus a little resourcefulness), good things happened to me every day in situations I never thought I would find myself.

What a wonderful world.

Homeward bound with Shorty
(photo by his sister Ginny Davis)

Parting Thoughts

A sampling of heroes

Willie

Barry

Ray

Doug

Jan

Jeff (Admin.)

BEING WITH YOU *(Song)*

Being with you meant living your nightmares
Wiping the sweat from your forehead as you lay sleeping
Taking the side of the bed between you and the door
Living with guilt
Living with afterwar silences
Faces of the ones who never came home.
living fast
moving fast
running fast
Trying to make up for no parades
Being with you meant knowing
you never stayed in one place too log
Loving you anyway
And that was the hardest part
Of being with you

Spouses
Roberta and Billie
Bad Ass Boots

WE ARE ALL REAL

Dog whisperers Franny & Ginny singing with Copper and Boots

INSPIRED
FLAVOR
FRESH
FROM

ABOUT THE AUTHOR

Diane Ford Craig is a former newspaper reporter, singer-songwriter, and graduate of New York University (B.A. 1983/M.A. 2005). She has won two journalism awards from the New Hampshire Press Association for feature writing and investigative reporting.

The proud mother of two grown children ("Susie & Fred"), she is band wife to lead guitarist "Jim Bob" Craig. Both are love slaves to Jax the Dawg, the canine poser on the cover of this book.

Large gift collection (15"W x 21.5"H) of 36 pin buttons (2.25") from this book is available for a limited time at **www.books2buttons.com** **or the alaskapress.store** **alaskapress@gmail.com**

Next book by Diane Ford Craig: ***CIRCLE OF FIFTHS*** A novel of intrigue set in Italy.

ISBN 978-1-886921-00-9